The Home Organizing Workbook

Clearing Your Clutter, Step by Step

By Meryl Starr

Photographs by Wendi Nordeck

CHRONICLE BOOKS
SAN FRANCISCO

Library of Congress Cataloging-in-Publication Data available.

ISBN: 0-8118-3732-7

Manufactured in China

Design by Efrat Rafaeli

Photo stylist: Anthony Albertus

Photo assistant: Deborah Sherman

Distributed in Canada by Raincoast Books
9050 Shaughnessy Street, Vancouver, British Columbia V6P 6E5

10 9 8 7 6 5 4 3

Chronicle Books LLC
85 Second Street, San Francisco, California 94105
www.chroniclebooks.com

CONTENTS

INTRODUCTION

Home organization is the great equalizer. A scrupulously clean person can have a spick-and-span but poorly organized home in which clearing off the dining room table becomes an all-day task, and much-needed items seem like buried treasure without the proverbial map. On the other hand, those on the sloppy side can maintain an impressively well-organized home, in which everything sits in its logical place, and each room is simple to clean and to keep clean. Whether you count yourself the former, the latter, or (most likely) somewhere in between, *The Home Organizing Workbook* can help you improve existing home-organizing systems and create new ones that will work for the long term. What ultimately determines good home organization is a system that works for you—a system that makes it easy for you to clear the clutter, streamline your busy life, and make your home a restful and nurturing place.

Home disorganization comes in many forms. An approach to organization that works for someone you know doesn't mean it will necessarily work for you and your family. An ill-fitting system can prevent you from accomplishing household tasks and your family from enjoying daily activities. At worst, it will promote, rather than remedy, the accumulation of clutter. Because your home-organizing problems are different from your neighbor's, you'll need to consider a variety of potential solutions.

The Home Organizing Workbook will help you assess your home's needs and find effective ways to meet them.

- **Are you unable to relax in your living areas because you're surrounded and distracted by piles of possessions?**

- **Do you suspect your closets and storage areas are filled with items that you don't even know you own?**

- **Do you keep things because you might need them later, then find you rarely look at them again—until you do look at them and declare you "might need them later"?**

- **Do you delay tidying up cluttered areas because you fear the task will turn into a long, involved project?**

- **Do you think that organizing your home is the same as cleaning it?**

If you answered yes to any of these questions, this book can help you by offering simple, step-by-step strategies for clearing the clutter.

No doubt about it—trying to change your habits can be overwhelming. To control the clutter in your home, however, you don't need to achieve and maintain a state of orderly perfection. Instead, you can begin in one room, or even an area of a room, and solve one problem at a time, one step at a time. In the process—with this workbook as your guide—you will develop systems that function best for your home and help ensure long-term success.

The Home Organizing Workbook walks you through each key room in your home, starting with the kitchen and ending with such storage areas as garages, basements, and attics. A simple questionnaire at the beginning of each chapter directs you to the hot spots that need attention. Once you've defined these problem areas, you can turn to the corresponding solutions. Each chapter also has step-by-step projects that help you jump-start the process of clearing the clutter. At the end is a list of indispensable organizing tools and accessories. An extensive resource guide at the back of the book puts these tools at your fingertips.

Now that you have *The Home Organizing Workbook* in hand, jettison any pressures to achieve organizational perfection. Turn to a chapter, go into a room, and explore the practical advice and handy solutions. It's time to get organized.

the **KITCHEN**

If your life is like most people's, the kitchen is probably the busiest room in your home.

Not only do you prepare and cook meals there, but you may also rely on the kitchen as a part-time office for opening mail and paying bills, maybe even for helping your kids with their homework. The kitchen is also the natural gathering place for entertaining guests. You don't want to straighten up every time you serve a meal or be in a panic before company arrives. There's no reason to give up any of your diverse uses of the kitchen. Reorganizing will help you make the room less cluttered and more functional.

The first step is to assess how you are currently using storage space, counter-tops, and other parts of your kitchen. Answer the brief questionnaire on page 16 to evaluate the problems you may need to solve. But if you have an itch to get started and don't want to tackle a major reorganization, you can begin with one of three simple projects that will make a big difference in your kitchen.

kitchen

questionnaire ✳ ✳ ✳

1 : **Are your cabinets so overstuffed that you don't know what you own—that maybe you do have a complete set of matching wineglasses or pasta bowls but can't always find them?**

2 : **Do you store appliances, pots, utensils, or items like cookbooks on the countertop or other surfaces because your cabinets are chock-full?**

If you answered yes to either question, you probably lack sufficient cabinet space, a common problem in small homes and apartments. Turn to page 21 for tips on maximizing limited cabinet storage.

3 : **Do you need to look through a number of cabinets before you find the right lid for a pan, the saucers that match your favorite cups, or an appliance you regularly use?**

4 : **After a shopping trip or when cleaning up after cooking a meal, do you put items in the nearest available cabinet rather than in a consistently designated place?**

Answering yes to either question may indicate that regardless of having adequate space, your cabinets may be in disarray. For advice on establishing good cabinet organization, go to page 23.

5 : **Although you want to put all your mixing spoons or all your cloth napkins and placemats in one place, or want to store other kitchen essentials out of sight, are you unable to find a drawer that will hold them?**

6 : **Do your drawers contain stationery and hardware supplies or other items that you do not use for meal preparation, while your countertop is littered with kitchen utensils?**

If you nodded yes to either of these questions, you probably lack adequate drawer space. For advice on maximizing limited drawer space or finding alternate storage solutions, turn to page 25.

7 : **Are your drawers so cluttered that you can't find the spatula you prefer to use, or the extra filters for your coffeemaker, or other kitchen tools you need daily?**

As with cabinets, not having enough drawers may not be your problem. If you answered yes to either question, you'll want to implement some of the drawer-organization strategies on page 27.

8 : **Are related items stored in separate drawers—aluminum foil in one drawer and plastic wrap in another, mixing spoons in one drawer and metal whisks in another?**

9 : **When you are preparing a meal, do the appliances and other kitchen tools on your counter get in the way?**

Responding yes to any of these questions indicates that you have insufficient counter space. Go to page 29 for solutions to this common problem.

10 : **Are you constantly cleaning up as you cook just to gain more counter space?**

11 : **When sharing the cooking with someone else in your family or with a guest, do you tend to run out of preparation space?**

12 : **Do you find that the most frequently used items are not easily accessible—that you need to traverse the kitchen too many times to assemble the cookware, utensils, and appliances you need to cook a meal?**

If you answered yes to either question, how you currently use your kitchen cabinets, drawers, counter space, and food storage does not promote smooth and efficient flow. Chances are that the cookware you use daily is not at your fingertips. Page 31 offers ideas for making improvements that will save you time and reduce frustration.

13 : **Is meal preparation taking much longer than you feel it should?**

14 : **Have you ever thought you had an ingredient for a recipe only to be unable to locate it in the refrigerator, freezer, or pantry?**

If you answered yes to any of these questions, you need a system for keeping track of food in your refrigerator, freezer, and pantry. For solutions, turn to page 33.

15 : **Do you buy duplicate condiments, canned goods, spices, or other foods because they are not stored where you can locate them easily?**

16 : **When you check packaged foods in your refrigerator, freezer, or pantry, are some past their pull date and therefore unusable?**

For many families, the kitchen is household headquarters. It's the place where everyone begins the day, and it's the place where they wind up after returning home. Your kitchen may be a repository of possessions that don't belong. If so, consider some of these solutions.

- Designate an empty bin or basket for magazines, toys, and other items that should not be stored in the kitchen. Assign one family member the job of regularly putting everything away.

- Find or create a space where family members can temporarily stash books, jackets, and other belongings when they come home from work or school. Then make a rule that everything should all be removed from the kitchen by dinnertime.

- Hang large envelopes or small baskets, or put bins or sorters on a shelf, and label one per family member. Use these containers to distribute paperwork, notes, and mail.

common Kitchen Problems

Now that you know the areas in your kitchen that need attention, it's time to focus on solutions. Some of following ideas will work for you; others may not be applicable to your situation. You will want to experiment with various solutions—and different storage accessories (page 42)—to find the best choices for your kitchen.

I don't have enough cabinet space.

The most obvious solution is to install more cabinets. If you can afford this endeavor but are unable to spare the wall space, consider adding cabinets near the ceiling. Out-of-reach storage is ideal for special-occasion china, glassware, or silverware and other infrequently used kitchenware. If new cabinets are not an option, an equally effective solution is maximizing the storage in your existing cabinets. You may want to try this before you go to the expense of purchasing and installing new cabinets.

Prior to embarking on the solutions on the following page, scrutinize the contents of your cabinets and pull out items you no longer need. Are you holding on to mismatched glasses or mugs that never leave the cabinet? Or lids that don't fit any of the pots in your collection? Or broken appliances that you once thought you'd have repaired? Disposing of them will free up valuable space. As you reorganize your cabinets, be sure that all of the items are near where you will use them. If you find that you need to improve the flow of your kitchen, see page 31.

Arrange by category. This is one of the essential rules of thumb for functional and efficient home organization. In general, store together items of a similar type, size, and shape. Stacking plates, keeping canned goods together, and nesting pans saves space and makes them easy to locate.

Turn to deep storage. Infrequently used dinnerware such as china and crystal or even appliances—say, the bread machine—can be boxed and kept in a garage, storage closet, or bedroom closet. Make a list of the items and their locations so you know where to find them later.

Adjust shelves. If possible, move shelves as you rearrange the cabinet contents. Start with the bottom of a cabinet and then adjust the shelf to accommodate the tallest item. Install the next shelf accordingly. Leave enough height to fit stackable items like plates and bowls, making sure that the shelves are sturdy enough to carry their weight.

Maximize cabinet interiors. Install hooks from cabinet shelves for hanging mugs and teacups or a rack for hanging stemmed glassware. Space can be left underneath for stacks of plates or bowls.

Compact and protect. Installing vertical cabinet dividers allows you to store cutting boards, serving trays, baking sheets, and wire racks vertically, rather than piled precariously on one another. Each divided section can hold two to four items. Cabinet dividers come in assorted sizes.

Stack smart. Pile plastic food-storage containers by size, from large to small, inside one another. Store matching lids in a separate pile, also by size. When choosing containers, keep in mind that square ones take up less room than round ones, thereby minimizing wasted space.

Call for backup. There are numerous varieties of organizers designed expressly for installation on the backs of cabinet doors. These organizers come in a variety of dimensions and will hold everything from utensils to jars of spices to lids for pots and pans. An organizer hung inside the door of the cabinet under your sink is perfect for sponges, scouring pads, rubber gloves, and detergent. Another type, a pull-down sink tray, is fitted behind the top, horizontal panel in front of the sink; the tray can accommodate sponges, scouring pads, and rubber gloves.

Go high. Pots and pans can be removed from cabinets and stored on a ceiling- or wall-mounted pot rack made specifically for this purpose. A wire basket hung from the ceiling can hold produce that is stored at room temperature.

Go to the wall. A wall-mounted sheet of pegboard with hooks can hold pots, pans, and utensils—often a good strategy for small apartment kitchens. Pegboard is usually brown but can be painted any color.

Add floor storage. Sturdy wooden or steel adjustable shelving can hold cookbooks, plates, baskets, large appliances, and bulk-food containers. Or you may prefer stacking baskets, which are practical containers for potatoes, onions, and other produce.

Even if you organized your cabinets six months or a year ago, don't be surprised if they are in disarray again. You may need to re-sort and reorganize every year or so as you acquire more kitchen equipment or change the way you like to cook.

Begin by opening all the cabinet doors. Then stand back and look at how the contents are arranged. Take time to visualize how you can improve the organization. Should baking pans be moved to a cabinet nearer to the stove, or all the baking sheets be stored alongside the bread pans? Or salad bowls placed under the counter where you always set the cutting board? Or oils and vinegars grouped near spices and herbs, rather than in a separate cabinet? Imagining in advance what would work best for you will save time when you start to rearrange. You may want to sketch out your new storage ideas and make additional changes as you consider the solutions on the following page.

tips Small children will appreciate being able to get out their own bowls, plates, and cups for meals or snacks. If the dishes are accessible, they may even get in the habit of putting everything away. Reserve a lower cabinet for this plastic ware. Many of the items are stackable and can be stored without taking up too much space. Kids' plastic utensils can be stashed in an open plastic container next to the dishware.

Organizing Solutions:

Arrange by category. Once you've outlined your plan, you want to remove everything from each cabinet and sort the items into categories. You will probably find things that did not belong in the cabinets where they were stored—or maybe chipped dishes, mismatched glasses, old cookware, or manuals for long-gone appliances that you no longer use or need. Make a separate pile for discards. By keeping like items together, you need remember only where to look for all pots and pans, or small appliances, or everyday dishes, or breakfast cereals, rather than where to search for each individual item.

Organize for efficiency. The best way to arrange dishware and cookware is by size and frequency of use. If you customarily set the dinner table with specific plates and glasses, store them together and within reach. Bowls for cereal, small glasses for juice, and mugs for coffee and tea should similarly be grouped together. Perhaps you entertain frequently and serve both wine and mixed drinks. In this case, you may want to designate a cabinet for the glasses you reserve for guests. On the other hand, if you bake only at the holidays, you can store your cake pans, cookie cutters, and related equipment in a less-accessible cabinet.

Store transparently. If you have loose packets of salad dressing mixes, powdered shakes, and tea bags, store them by category in clear plastic storage containers. You'll be able to see what you have without rummaging through the cabinet.

Group ingredients. All similar ingredients should be stored together, and those that you use frequently, such as dried herbs, spices, oils, vinegars, and condiments, should be where you can reach them easily. Use lazy Susans, spice racks, or shelf expanders to help you keep the items in order and use cabinet space efficiently. To reorganize your spice cabinet, see the quick-and-easy project on page 34.

Containerize and label. Transfer all dry goods, such as pasta, sugar, flours, and grains, into plastic, glass, or stainless-steel canisters. Use tape and permanent marker to label the contents and include the date. Review the dates occasionally and replace the contents if more than six months old. Round and square canisters are available; square works best by maximizing the use of available space.

Update drawers. Install pull-out drawers in bottom cabinets. Often designed to replace existing shelves, pull-out drawers on runners make it easy to reach what is stored deep within cabinets.

Avoid avalanches. If you have a broom closet in the kitchen, use holders mounted on the back of the door to secure brooms and mops so they won't fall out when you open the door. Some holders can also accommodate vacuum cleaner tubes and the flexible hose. With these tools mounted on the door rather than taking up interior space, you can install additional shelving, hooks, and dispensers for cleaning products, rags, plastic bags, and buckets.

Spread the word. Use tape and permanent marker to label all the cabinet shelves. Now family members know exactly where to put everything.

I don't have enough drawer space.

Most people face this dilemma at some point. It's a natural impulse to keep stuffing utensils, napkins, and other supplies in kitchen drawers until space runs out. Once you sort through the contents and reorganize the drawers according to the solutions on the following page, you'll be surprised at the extra space gained.

tips

When you entertain family and friends, it's much more fun to have them in the kitchen, rather than asking them to wait for you in the dining or living room. If your kitchen lacks space to accommodate guests, one of these solutions might work.

- If you have a center island, arrange stools around it. Guests can be served drinks and appetizers while you prepare the main meal.

- In a spacious kitchen, add a small couch or some comfortable chairs along one wall. You can also add a small table for drinks and snacks, whether you leave it there permanently or pull it out only when you have company.

- Install a permanent bench under a window or in a corner. You can consider an enclosed bench whose seat or front opens to provide storage for such items as napkins, tablecloths, trivets, and candles and their holders.

• **Arrange by category.** Start by pulling out all the items from drawers and looking for things that you no longer use or need—such as utensils with broken handles, or old dish towels or cloth napkins that are best delegated as rags. In many households, kitchen drawers contain general supplies such as lightbulbs and batteries or tools such as pliers and screwdrivers. If you are short on drawer space, try to find a better place for these items in the laundry or utility room, garage, or basement.

• **Gang or hang utensils.** If you have enough counter space, store long-handled wooden spoons and utensils such as spatulas and ladles in a crock or a stable vase or pitcher near the stove. Another option is to hang utensils from hooks or racks mounted near the stove. Both solutions free up drawer space and put utensils within reach.

• **Go portable.** A freestanding utensils holder or tote can be used to store forks, knives, and spoons for everyday use. This portable caddy can be set on the counter or kitchen table and can even be tucked out of the way in a cabinet.

• **Call for backup.** Hooks installed inside a cabinet door are great for hanging measuring spoons, measuring cups, and other small items that you want to keep out of sight. If you have a large cabinet, hooks inside the door are perfect for hanging placemats held by binder clips. Kitchen-wrap caddies and dispensers mount on the backs of cabinet doors and hold aluminum foil, plastic wrap, and waxed paper.

• **Add shelving.** A hanging wire shelf mounted under an upper cabinet is useful for stacking napkins, linens, and dish towels but does not inhibit use of the counter.

• **Hang cutlery.** If you lack drawer space for the knives you use for food preparation, install a magnetic strip made specifically for cutlery on the wall behind a counter. Make sure that no one can accidentally bump into the knives and that they are not reachable by children.

• **Go to the wall.** Near the stove, alongside the sink, or above the counter, look for spots where you can tuck hooks for hanging potholders, dish towels, and even spare sets of keys.

I have plenty of drawer space, but everything is in disarray.

Over time, it's easy for drawers to become crammed with a jumble of utensils, kitchen tools, and other kitchen essentials. You can actually fit more in drawers if they are organized— and not have such a hard time finding what you need. Some of the solutions on the following page and the products on page 42 are certain to work for your kitchen.

• **Arrange by category.** There is no better first step than making sure that all related items are stored together—all aluminum foil, plastic wrap, and sandwich bags; all baking tools and cake-decorating supplies; all everyday tableware.

• **Divide and conquer.** Use partitioned cutlery trays and drawer dividers to organize tableware and utensils. These trays and dividers are available in a range of sizes and with a variety of compartments. If storing knives in a drawer, cover the blades with knife guards to prevent the cutting edges from becoming dull and to prevent accidents when you reach into the drawer.

• **Avoid overstuffing.** Even if you install partitioned trays and drawer dividers, try not to cram them full. Now that you've gained space, leave room for future acquisitions.

• **File paperwork.** Appliance warranties do not need to be stored in a kitchen drawer—or anywhere else in the kitchen. Discard warranties for appliances you no longer own and store current documents in a file cabinet. Recipes and magazine clippings are easier to access if kept in a binder on a shelf. A box with dividers is better for storing recipes than keeping them loose in a drawer.

• **Control the miscellaneous.** If you can devote a drawer to odds and ends such as rubber bands, twist-ties, labeling tape, and pens, use a drawer divider to keep the different items separate. Lock-top plastic bags and small, clear plastic containers are also good for this purpose.

tips

Reorganizing drawers presents an opportunity to clean the insides and install removable plastic mesh or rubberized liners. The liners cushion the contents and keep them from moving around. They also prevent drawers from getting scratched, encourage air circulation, and allow dust and dirt to fall to the drawer bottom.

I don't have enough counter space.

Lack of sufficient counter space can be one of the most frustrating kitchen problems. If your kitchen is large enough, you might consider structural changes such as installing a center island, which adds both work surface and cabinet storage. You'll need about six square feet of floor space for the island, plus sufficient room around the island for traffic flow and for accessing major appliances and bottom cabinets. A less-costly option, especially for apartments, is installing a custom-made, flip-up countertop on an empty wall. Find someone with a little carpentry experience to install this counter, which does double duty for food preparation and eating, and can be folded out of the way when not in use.

Before you contemplate an ambitious and potentially costly project, try maximizing your existing counters by implementing the solutions on the following page.

tips

Coffee grinders, handheld electric mixers, electric can openers—you use them frequently and need to find the best place to keep them so they're always at the ready. One of these options will work for your kitchen. Remember to store accessories alongside or near the appliance.

- Plenty of counter space? Keep appliances on the counter near an electrical outlet.

- Enough cabinet space? Store all small appliances on a large lazy Susan. A quick turn and what you need is at your fingertips.

- Short on counter or cabinet space? Choose appliances that can be mounted for permanent use or storage underneath the cabinet, leaving the counter free. Install a small shelf for appliances on the wall between cabinet and counter, near an electrical outlet, or retrofit an awkward, empty corner where your countertop meets the wall with an appliance garage.

Organizing Solutions:

- **Go portable.** Purchase a rolling cart with a butcher-block top for food preparation. Many carts have shelves and drawers for storage. Some come with towel racks, or racks can be added.

- **Lift appliances.** Especially if you need to replace appliances, look for a coffeemaker, can opener, or toaster oven that can be mounted on the bottom of a wall cabinet. Keep the overall kitchen flow in mind when you install them.

- **Add shelving.** If your upper cabinets are mounted sufficiently above your counter, you can install small shelves underneath them to hold cookbooks, small appliances, jars of spices and herbs, or other items you want to have handy.

- **Elevate cookbooks.** Rather than use up counter space by laying a cookbook flat when in use, prop it up in a cookbook holder, which takes up less space.

- **Emphasize versatility.** Use a large cutting board made to fit over the sink. The dish rack and dish drainer, especially if foldable, can be moved out of the way during meal preparation.

- **Gang and hang utensils.** Consider mounting a small, horizontal steel grid or rod to your wall. Fitted with hooks, this becomes a convenient location for hanging large cooking utensils within easy reach.

- **Go high.** Hang a three-tier basket from the ceiling to hold items you normally keep on the counter, such as gadgets, utensils, and produce. The top of the refrigerator is an overlooked storage area, suitable for a small collection of cookbooks buttressed by sturdy bookends or a box or binder of recipes.

---

tips

Even if your drawers and cabinets are jam-packed, clutter-free countertops can make you feel as if your kitchen is under control. You may choose to defer the task of reorganizing your hidden storage, but try to take a hard look at your counters every week to make sure nothing is interfering with meal preparation and cooking. Remove appliances that you do not use frequently, stow pots in the oven when it's not in use, and find an alternative display area for decorative objects. The counter is best reserved for the cooking essentials you use daily.

My kitchen doesn't seem to be convenient for cooking and other kitchen tasks. I always feel that I'm running from one end of the room to the other just to cook a simple meal.

No problem gets to the heart of home organization faster than a room that lacks flow. Flow—the ability to have things at your fingertips where and when you need them—can be more important to working successfully in the kitchen than to any other room in your home. When pans and lids, cutting boards and knives, and your collection of favorite recipes are placed where you can access them with ease, you no longer have to scramble frantically back and forth across the room to find them. You'll discover that meal preparation and cooking are more efficient and stress free. Because lack of effective flow is such a common problem, it can be a good idea to analyze this aspect of your kitchen before reorganizing cabinets, drawers, and food storage, just in case major improvements are in order.

tips Keep single dollar bills in a can or jar on the counter or an accessible kitchen shelf for tipping the pizza delivery person or as daily milk or snack money for the kids.

Arrange by category. If you go away with only one new rule to organize by it is to store similar items together. Each category—be it grains and pastas, herbs and spices, wineglasses, serving ware, food-storage containers—should be grouped together in a designated place rather than scattered throughout the kitchen.

Store at arm's reach. A key rule of thumb is to keep items close to where they are used. Place pots, pans, and lids near the stove; coffee mugs near the coffeemaker; knives near the cutting board. If possible, dishes, plates, and glasses should be stored in a cabinet near the dishwasher or sink, making for easy loading and unloading.

Make essentials accessible. Items that you use frequently—salt and pepper for seasoning; aluminum foil and plastic wrap; versatile utensils, such as wooden spoons; and everyday frying pans and saucepans—should be within reach.

Banish clutter. Always keep counters free of items you do not absolutely need for daily meal preparation. Appliances, knives, and cutting boards can be stored in drawers, cabinets, or shelves directly above or below the work surface where they are generally used.

Go portable. A rolling cart with a butcher-block top for food preparation, a caddy for storing daily tableware, and a portable stand for paper towels may improve your kitchen flow by allowing you to move them where and when they are needed, but place them out of traffic when they are not.

Collect recipes. Handwritten recipes or those printed from a computer can be organized in a three-ring binder by course, ingredient, and occasion for convenient reference. Recipes clipped from magazines and newspapers can be enclosed in plastic sleeves in the binder or filed in a recipe box. If you save entire magazines, find an out-of-the-way place to store them, rather than taking up valuable counter or cabinet space.

Hide trash. Storing the trash can in a cabinet will free up floor space. Pull-out units, which make the trash accessible, can also hold receptacles for compost and recycling.

Think safety. Heavy cookware like roasting pans, glass baking dishes and casseroles, and cast-iron frying pans, along with hefty appliances like stand mixers and food processors, are best kept in low cabinets, close to the floor. Lighter items like dinnerware and glasses can go in high cabinets. You don't want to reach above your head for something heavy.

I can't keep track of the food items I have on hand, and sometimes food spoils before I can use it.

You know the scenarios all too well. You rush into the pantry to get a box of pasta, only to remember that you ran out last week and forgot to add it to your shopping list. Or you dig into the produce drawer and find that the greens and tomatoes you intended to make into a salad are suitable strictly for the compost heap. Or you pull out a package of frozen fruit from the freezer and realize it was put there a year ago. With some reorganization and occasional maintenance of your refrigerator, freezer, and pantry, you'll have what you need on hand, be able to find it, and waste less food.

- **Arrange by category.** Some items, such as small containers of spreads, can be tucked into refrigerator drawers; others, such as condiments and sauces, are best stored on the refrigerator door. Apply the same approach to the freezer. In your pantry, place all the cereals, all the canned goods, and all the pastas together. If necessary, break a grouping into separate categories, such as cereals into hot and cold or canned goods into meats and vegetables.

- **Create a pantry.** Not every home has a built-in pantry. If your kitchen is lacking, designate a large cabinet or pair of cabinets as your pantry.

- **Sort and discard.** Clean out the refrigerator at least once a week, and your freezer every month, and dispose of spoiled foods and items you do not plan on eating. Do the same for your pantry every month or two—or when you sense that the space is getting cluttered and things are hard to find.

- **Store transparently.** Deli foods, such as meats, and various snacks can be stored in clear plastic containers in the refrigerator. Keep small pieces of cheese in containers so they stay fresh and are easy to find.

- **Containerize and label.** Use plastic, glass, or stainless-steel canisters to hold grains, flour, sugar, and similar ingredients. Label them—being sure to include the date—using masking tape and permanent marker, or a label maker. Also label and date leftovers and other foods stored in the freezer.

- **Avoid overstuffing.** Make sure you can see all the items in your pantry, refrigerator, and freezer. If you try to fit too much, items in the back get forgotten. But if you have no choice but to fill the refrigerator, freezer, or pantry to capacity, make a list of the foods in the back and post it nearby. You can also use a lazy Susan in the refrigerator or a pantry shelf so foods won't get lost.

- **Anticipate restocking.** A pad of paper and pen mounted on the front or side of the refrigerator or in the pantry can be dedicated to listing foods that need replacing the next time you go shopping. When you use the last of the canned tomatoes or mustard or eggs, immediately add them to the list. If you have pantry space, purchase extra dry goods so you know you have backup.

Organize Your Spice Cabinet

Time required: 30 minutes – 1 hour

Two lynchpins of home organization apply to this project: Store at arm's reach, and arrange by category. Ideally, your spices and herbs should be kept close to where you customarily prepare meals. You'll also want to group everything based on what you use and how you cook. Perhaps you want to separate seasonings into the savory and the sweet, or you simply want to keep all herbs together and all spices together. If you have a large collection that you will be storing in rows, alphabetizing might be the preferred system. To make efficient use of space, consider purchasing accessories such a spice rack for a wall or countertop, a lazy Susan for a cabinet shelf, or a spice organizer for a drawer.

1   Collect your spices, dried herbs, and other seasonings and put them on a counter or table.

2   Sort through the various products and discard any that are more than six months old. Save any jars or tins that are reusable; wash and dry them. Add to your shopping list the spices and herbs you need to replace.

3   If any seasonings need new containers, use a funnel to transfer them to clean jars or tins. Label and date all of the containers.

4   Install your rack, lazy Susan, or organizer and arrange your spices and herbs.

You will need all or some of the following:

Garbage bag

Shopping list and pen

Blank labels or masking tape and permanent marker, or label maker

New empty jars or tins

Funnel

Accessories such as spice rack, lazy Susan, or spice organizer

Maintenance Strategies

Store herbs and spices away from heat and light to preserve freshness and flavor. Replace them after six months.

After using a spice, always put it back in the same spot.

Put a seasoning on your shopping list before you run out.

If a jar or tin is empty and you don't yet have a replacement, leave the container where it is and put the item on your shopping list. Replace the empty container with the new one after you go shopping.

Organize Your Pantry

Time required: 2 hours

If you're not fortunate enough to have a walk-in pantry, you can easily create one by using a large cabinet or pair of smaller cabinets, making sure the food storage is conveniently located near the area where you prepare meals. Before you start, decide if you need any accessories, such as lazy Susans, hanging shelves, or stacking baskets.

1   Empty the pantry and set everything on a table or counter.

2   Go through all the items, from cans of soup and packages of flour to bags of chips and boxes of cereal. Discard products that are stale, spoiled, or will not be used. Add to your shopping list any foods or ingredients that you want to replace.

3   If necessary, clean the pantry shelves, walls, and door. You may also want to cover the shelves with liners.

4   Use the canisters to store such ingredients as flours, sugars, pastas, dried fruits, grains, and beans. Label and date each canister. If you have small loose items such as hot chocolate mixes or teabags, store them in plastic storage containers.

Continued →

You will need all or some of the following:

Garbage bags

Shopping list and pen

Cleaning supplies

Shelf liner

Plastic, glass, or stainless-steel canisters

Blank labels or masking tape and permanent marker, or label maker

Clear plastic storage containers

Lazy Susans, stacking baskets, freestanding shelf units, hanging storage racks or shelves for wall or door

Step stool

5   This next step is key: Divide the items into cate-
     gories before reshelving, so you can keep like items
     together and avoid rummaging to find what you
     want. If necessary, experiment with the groupings
     until they seem appropriate for how you cook.

6   Take a good look at what you are planning to put
     back in the pantry. Decide on which items should
     be the most accessible and which are used less
     frequently. Juice packs and snacks for your children
     can be stowed in stacking baskets on a low shelf.
     Potatoes, onions, garlic, and other essential ingre-
     dients can go in baskets near the front of a middle
     shelf, where they are in easy reach. Cake mixes for
     special occasions are best stored on a high shelf
     reachable by a step stool. Baking powder, baking
     soda, and other small containers can go on wall or
     door shelves, or on a lazy Susan. If necessary,
     sketch out your plan on paper.

7   Once you are satisfied with your plan, install any
     accessories and return all the items to the pantry.

Maintenance Strategies

Always put items back in the spot
where you found them.

Keep a pad and pencil in or near
the pantry so you can list foods you
need to replace before they run out.

Go through the pantry every
month or two to remind yourself
what you have—and to make any
better arrangements.

Label the contents of shelves with
masking tape and permanent marker,
or with a label maker. Other members
of the household can get used to putting things back where they belong.

| tips | Store plastic bags from the supermarket in a plastic bag holder, conve-
niently designed to recycle and dispense those shopping bags that pile
up, in the broom closet or behind the closet door. The bags will be neatly
tucked out of sight but ready when you need one. |

One of the key home-organization rules of thumb is to store items close to where you will be using them. If you have a drawer near your stove, that's where you want to stash wooden spoons, spatulas, and other cooking utensils you need for preparing most meals. You probably prefer one area of the counter for cutting and chopping vegetables. The drawer directly underneath is the best place to store knives and tools such as swivel-blade vegetable peelers, flat graters, and citrus zesters. If you store your good knives in a drawer, be sure to outfit them with knife guards so the blades do not get dull and you don't hurt yourself when reaching into the drawer.

Organizing the Refrigerator and Freezer

Time required: 2 hours

A tidy refrigerator and freezer will make meal preparation easier and cut down on wasted food. Before embarking on this project, think about any storage accessories you might want to add to the refrigerator, like a lazy Susan or plastic storage containers. You might want to refer to your refrigerator manual. Manufacturers sell handy accessories for storage of specific items such as wine bottles.

1   Tackle the refrigerator and freezer separately. Transfer the contents of the refrigerator to a counter or table.

2   Foods that are spoiled or will never be used should be discarded. Add to your shopping list anything you want to replace. Store any perishables in a cooler while your work.

3   Remove the shelves and drawers from the refrigerator and clean them with glass cleaner or a cleaning solution approved for your refrigerator. If necessary, vacuum the air vents and grills under and behind the refrigerator. Check the temperature setting and make sure it is correct; this information is in your manual.

4   Divide foods into categories: dairy products, fresh meats and fish, cheese, condiments, fruits, vegetables, and beverages. Make sure that food is stored in appropriately sized containers. Large, incompletely filled Jars hog space. It you have large jars partly filled with olives, for example, transfer them to smaller containers.

You will need all or some of the following:

Garbage bags

Shopping list and pen

Cooler

Cleaning supplies, including glass cleaner

Vacuum cleaner

Jars and plastic storage containers

Lazy Susans

Blank labels or masking tape and permanent marker, or label maker

2 boxes of baking soda

5   You may want to adjust the shelves to accommodate certain categories. If you want to keep drinks like soda in bottles and orange juice in cartons on the top shelf, adjust the shelf as necessary.

6   Return food items to the refrigerator, keeping your categories intact and following these rules of thumb: Frequently used items like milk or juice should be stored toward the front of the refrigerator. The shelves inside the door are ideal for grouping condiments—ketchup with mustard, pickles with peppers, jams with jellies. Fruits and vegetables go in the designated temperature-controlled drawers. Fresh meats and fish and other highly perishable items belong on the bottom shelf, the coldest area of the refrigerator. Cheeses and deli meats can be stored in their own drawer or in separate clear plastic containers. Use lazy Susans to gang small containers.

7   Repeat steps 1 through 6 for the freezer. Label and date everything before you return it to the freezer. Keep butter and frozen meals in the door or near the front. Like items, such as meats, can be grouped together on the shelves.

8   Write the date on the baking soda boxes and open them. Put one box in the freezer, the other in the refrigerator. The baking soda, which absorbs odors, should be replaced every three months.

Maintenance Strategies

Always put foods back in the areas and with the categories where they belong.

Clean out your refrigerator before you go food shopping for the week. You will see what you have used and what you need to buy. Regular cleaning—weekly for the refrigerator, monthly for the freezer—helps keep everything organized.

Keep a magnetic pad on the refrigerator with a pen attached for your ongoing shopping list. Try to write down foods you need to restock before they run out.

| tips | Hang a large wall calendar and a magnetic-clip pen on the refrigerator to keep track of events, meetings, doctor appointments, and birthdays and other special occasions. |

The following accessories, mentioned throughout the chapter, are relatively inexpensive and can be found in hardware and houseware stores.

- **Cabinet dividers.** These vertical dividers slip into your cabinets to organize flat items like baking sheets and cutting boards.

- **Cabinet door racks.** These racks made of plastic-coated wire are mounted on the inside of cabinet doors for holding plastic wrap, aluminum foil, and plastic bags.

- **Canisters and food-storage containers.** Made of glass, plastic, or stainless-steel, round or square canisters in a range of heights and capacities are an efficient way to store pastas, grains, cereals, flours, and other dried foods. Clear plastic containers are useful for storing food in the refrigerator or pantry.

- **Cookbook holders.** One of the most popular is an acrylic holder that keeps a cookbook upright and protects it while you cook.

- **Coupon organizer.** Coupons can be sorted and filed by category in this wallet-style holder.

- **Cutlery trays and drawer dividers.** These flat, partitioned trays fit in drawers and keep knives and utensils organized. They are available in many sizes, styles, and colors, some with two tiers for deep drawers. Measure the inside dimensions of drawers—height, depth, and width—before shopping.

- **Freestanding shelves.** Usually made of wood or steel (in chrome or black), these units are open on all sides and generally have adjustable shelves. They can be used for everything from cookbooks and appliances to plates and bulk-food containers.

- **Hooks.** Many sizes and styles are available, ideal for hanging mugs and cups inside a cabinet, utensils on the back of a cabinet door, and dish towels and potholders on the wall.

- **Kitchen-wrap caddies.** These wall-mounted holders are perfect for storing several boxes of kitchen wrap, such as aluminum foil, plastic wrap, and waxed paper.

- **Knife guards.** These slim, slip-on guards do double duty, protecting knives from dulling in the drawer and protecting fingers reaching in.

- **Lazy Susans.** Available in many diameters, these rotating trays are good for corner cabinets, can be used in the refrigerator and pantry, and are excellent for holding spices. Tall cabinets can accommodate Lazy Susans with more than one tier.

- **Lid organizers and holders.** Mounted on a door or wall, these plastic accessories hold any type of lid.

Magnetic knife strip. These strong magnetic strips hold the knife blades securely. Made in different lengths, the strip is mounted on the wall for keeping cutlery handy near a work surface.

Pegboard. Regularly spaced holes in this sheet of pressed wood accommodate hooks for hanging pots, pans, and utensils. The pegboard can be painted any color.

Plastic bag holder. The container takes up little space and allows you to reach in and retrieve one bag at a time.

Plastic-coated wire shelves. These handy and inexpensive units create multiple levels within cabinets. Before shopping, measure your cabinet as well as the height of the tallest item you plan to store beneath the shelving.

Pot rack. A rack suspended from the ceiling or mounted on the wall has hooks for hanging pots, pans, and cooking utensils.

Pull-down sink trays. Sponges, rubber gloves, scrapers, and scouring pads can be stored in these trays, which go behind the panel just below the sink. The panel is removed, the tray is installed, and the panel is replaced so that it flips open to reveal the tray.

Pull-out drawers. Installed in bottom cabinets, often replacing existing shelves, these drawers on runners make it easy to reach what is stored deep within cabinets.

Pull-out trash baskets. Also installed in bottom cabinets, especially those under the sink, these trash baskets keep garbage behind closed doors, sliding out for easy access.

Shelf expanders. Expanders are tiered shelves made of plastic or chrome that can be adjusted to increase storage space in a cabinet.

Spice racks and organizers. The various types include drawer organizers and hanging wall racks, as well as lazy Susans or turntables.

Stacking baskets. These baskets sit on the floor or on a shelf and stack vertically atop one another. They are perfect for storing potatoes, onions, fruits, and vegetables, as well as various pantry items.

Stemware rack. This rack is installed underneath an interior cabinet shelf. Stemmed glassware hangs upside down from the rack, leaving room underneath for additional storage.

Three-tier wire basket. The unit hangs from the ceiling, and the baskets, in progressively larger sizes from top to bottom, can hold an array of objects, including utensils, kitchen gadgets, and napkins.

Undershelf baskets. These plastic-coated wire baskets hang from a shelf to create storage space directly underneath.

Utensil caddies. A portable countertop caddy holds utensils upright. They are available in many styles and sizes.

the **DINING ROOM**

Although your dining room may not call out for as much reorganization as your kitchen or home office, it does invite multiple uses and can accumulate clutter.

The dining table is often a convenient place for family members to spread out special projects or deposit toys, magazines, books, and mail. If you have an eat-in kitchen, days or weeks may go by when the dining table is not needed for serving meals—until you want to entertain company. Regardless of your situation, a well-organized dining room can remain a functional and comfortable space for many uses, including enjoying meals with family and guests.

If you feel that your dining room could be better organized, answer the brief questionnaire on page 48 to assess the problems you may need to remedy. If you don't want to embark on a major overhaul, you can start with one of the two simple projects (pages 56 and 59) that may solve some of your most persistent problems.

Dining Room

questionnaire ✳ ✳ ✳

1 : **Does the clutter that accumulates during the week—mail, newspapers, homework, toys—often wind up on the dining room table?**

2 : **Do you have to take time to clean off the table just to serve a meal?**

3 : **Do you eat in the kitchen or another room because the table is hidden under clutter?**

If you have answered yes to any of these questions, your dining room is not being used for its intended purpose. You would be surprised at the number of households that share this problem. For solutions, turn to page 51.

4 : **Do you store linens, china, crystal, silverware, and serving ware in other parts of the house rather than in the dining room?**

5 : **Are all of the cabinets and other storage in the dining room filled to capacity?**

If you responded yes to either question, you probably aren't making efficient use of the storage potential in your dining room. On page 53, you'll find suggestions for improving your storage.

6 : **When you set the dining room table, is it difficult to find everything you need?**

7 : **Do you buy candles, party napkins, and other items over and over because you forget where you put them?**

8 : **Before guests arrive, do you spend too much time searching for your best linen tablecloth and napkins, then ultimately find them rumpled up in the back of the dining room cabinets or drawers?**

If yes is the answer to any of these questions, you are not using your available storage efficiently, even though you may have sufficient cabinet space. The solutions on page 55 will help you rethink your way of organizing.

Common Dining Room Problems

Having identified the areas of your dining room that need work, you are ready to review the organizing solutions on the following pages and choose those that will be best for your situation. You'll also want to look at the organizing accessories on page 63 and select those best suited to your dining room.

I don't use my dining room as a dining room.

There's no reason you can't have it both ways—using your dining table to work on a sewing project (or to spread out the Sunday paper) *and* to entertain family and friends, even on a moment's notice. What you need are a few simple strategies for preventing accumulations of clutter, like the ones on the following page.

Banish clutter. This is the persistent problem in most households—the dining table becomes a repository for magazines and newspapers and a work surface for paying bills and other tasks, then the clutter lingers until the day guests are expected. It's fine to use the dining table for other purposes, but consider making a household rule that all papers need to be removed and filed elsewhere after paying bills, or magazines and newspapers can be read at the table but must be placed in a specific place when the reader is done. If the accumulation is particularly daunting, you may want to do the project on page 56.

Give assignments. If you have trouble deciding where to move dining table clutter, designate particular places for distributing the various items. Magazines and newspapers can go in a rack, basket, or bin in the living room or another room where you are likely to read them. Baskets or bins, one per family member, can be set in the bedrooms for depositing mail, toys, and personal belongings. If you have a home office or a desk in another room where you pay bills, dedicate containers or organizers for incoming mail and bills yet to be paid.

Make the room special. When you've cleaned off the dining table, you can add a vase with fresh flowers or other decorative centerpiece such as candleholders with brand-new candles. This will remind family members that the table is a special place reserved for family meals and entertaining.

I don't have enough storage space in my dining room.

Dining rooms often feature a key piece of furniture such as a sideboard, hutch, or armoire that is used for storage, especially since many dining rooms do not have closets. Even if your dining room is small, it might be able to accommodate one of these practical pieces or another accessory that will increase your storage capacity. If you already have one or more pieces of furniture, go through all the cabinets and shelves, remove items that do not need to be in the dining room, and store them elsewhere. You may realize that tableware you use regularly really belongs in the kitchen, where you serve meals during the week.

tips
If your dining room table has its extra leaves in, but you don't really need all that space every day, consider taking them out and storing them in an out-of-the-way area. A little extra square footage in the dining room might make room for a portable storage unit for everyday use. Just roll it away when it's time to expand the table.

Turn to deep storage. You may have infrequently used items like holiday table decorations or heirlooms that are taking up much-needed space in the dining room. If this is the case, pack them in boxes, label the boxes, and move them to a storage closet, a high shelf in a bedroom closet, or your garage or attic. Keep a list of the boxes and their contents, noting their locations.

Relocate nearby. If you are storing tablecloths and napkins in the dining room, free up space for dishes and glasses by putting the tablecloths on hangers in a closet adjacent to the dining room or stowing them, with their matching napkins, in a linen closet. Draping the hanging tablecloths with plastic bags from the dry cleaner will keep them clean and pressed and let you see what you have on hand. If the closet has enough floor space, install a portable drawer storage unit for holding tableware, napkins, and other dining-table necessities.

Add or replace furniture. If your budget permits, trade in your current hutch, sideboard, or armoire for a taller one that will hold more but takes up the same amount of floor space. Or consider a piece that fits into the corner of the room and takes up less space than a wall piece. Another option is placing an attractive trunk alongside a wall or in a corner. Depending on its size and proportions, the trunk can hold a range of items, from trays and linens to candlesticks and candles. Be sure that any furniture you add will not crowd the dining room or interrupt the flow of traffic.

Add shelving. If your dining room cannot accommodate large pieces of furniture, and you're in need of additional storage space for tableware, it may be appropriate to add individual shelving units or wall-mounted shelves or cabinets. You can also install a single shelf up high—at about the level of picture molding—along an entire wall, or around the entire room, for the display of decorative items and attractive serving pieces.

Emphasize versatility. An enclosed bench with a lift-up seat can provide not only extra storage but also extra seating.

Go to the wall. Use open wall space to hang serving plates, bowls, and other handsome pieces. Special wire hangers are made to hold ceramic bowls and plates. Items that are accessible are more likely to be used.

Rack it up. If you store bottles of wine in a dining-room cabinet, consider using a wine rack instead. Small racks can be set on top of a large piece of furniture. Large racks are freestanding. Using a rack will free up cabinet space and prevent you from forgetting what is in your wine inventory.

I have plenty of storage space, but I can never find things when I need them.

If you can't find what you need for serving meals, chances are that the cabinets and drawers in your dining room furniture contain items that don't need to be kept in the dining room. Empty all of your hidden storage and decide which items are best stored in the kitchen or pantry— and which are seldom used and best relegated to deep storage. Then start reorganizing, using the solutions on the following page.

- **Arrange by category.** Always follow this rule of thumb for functional and efficient home organization by storing together items of a similar type, shape, and size. For instance, table linens, cloth napkins, and place mats should be kept in one place, as should candles and their holders. Crystal stemware goes with crystal glasses; china plates and bowls, with their matching serving pieces. Place all carving equipment in the same drawer. You may want to divide items by frequency of use—tableware for daily meals in one location (if you regularly eat in the dining room), items for entertaining or special occasions in another. With this system of organization, you need remember only where the category is stored, not where each individual item is kept.

- **Divide and conquer.** Sort and store silver and silver-plated tableware in cutlery trays lined with velvet, felt, or another soft fabric. This prevents the pieces from getting scratched as well as keeps them organized.

- **Containerize and protect.** Store good china and glassware in quilted china storage containers. These padded containers come in sizes appropriate for plates, bowls, saucers, cups, and stemware, and protect them from dust and from getting chipped and cracked.

- **Control the miscellaneous.** Dedicate a drawer to small items such as matches, napkin rings, and place cards. Arranging them in drawer dividers or putting them in clear plastic containers will prevent the drawer contents from becoming a jumble.

tips

Special silver-protector bags are available for storing silver trays, platters, and candlesticks. The bags both prevent the silver from tarnishing and prevent the items from getting scratched.

Reorganizing Dining Room Storage

Time required: 2–3 hours

Many dining rooms have one substantial piece of furniture, such as a sideboard, hutch, or armoire, with cabinets and drawers for storing cutlery, dishes, glassware, and serving pieces. Reorganizing the contents may gain extra space and also make everything you need more accessible. Before you start the project, review the list of accessories on page 63 and choose those best suited to your piece of furniture and the items you are storing.

1   Remove everything from your sideboard, hutch, or armoire. Chipped glassware and broken dishes that are beyond repair should be discarded. You may find serving ware or candlesticks, for instance, that you no longer use but are in good condition and can be given away. Seldom-used items such as platters pulled out only on holidays or other special occasions can be boxed carefully and stored elsewhere if cabinet space is limited.

2   Clean the shelves and drawers. With the piece of furniture empty, this is a good time to clean the interior thoroughly and install drawer and shelf liners.

3   Organize china, silverware, and other items by category before you return them to the shelves and drawers. Separate everyday items from those used infrequently.

You will need all or some of the following:

Garbage bags

Cleaning supplies

Drawer and shelf liners

Quilted china-storage containers

Fabric-lined cutlery trays

Silver-protector bags

Drawer dividers

4   Put your good china and stemware in quilted storage containers. If you have silver or silver-plated tableware, place it in a fabric-lined cutlery tray that will fit inside a drawer. Use the silver-protector bags for silver or silver-plated bowls, trays, and other serving ware. Install drawer dividers to help keep candles and other small objects tidy.

5   Put everything back, one item at a time. Frequently used dishes and tableware should be placed where they are easily accessed. China and silverware brought out for special occasions can go on top or bottom shelves, or toward the back.

Maintenance Strategies

Remember—put items used infrequently up high or out of the way. Put items used frequently at eye level.

Go through your cabinet once a year and get rid of items that you haven't used in the last twelve months.

When putting away china and silverware after a special occasion, take the opportunity to reorganize your hutch or cabinet.

| tips |

In many homes, freeing up the dining room table is the task that makes the biggest impact on improving the appearance and functionality of the dining room as a whole. The goal is not only to clear the table but also to organize so everything can be put away properly—rather than just relocating the piles of paperwork and other clutter. If this is your problem, turn to the solutions on page 51. Below you will find a few simple, long-term strategies for keeping the table clear of clutter.

- Never use the dining room table as a final resting place. It's fine to read the morning paper while enjoying your morning coffee, or to spread out a project temporarily, but when you're done, remove everything so the table is just as you found it.

- Decorate the table with a vase of flowers or other centerpiece such as candlesticks with candles. This can help to remind everyone in the family not to leave other things on the table.

- Make it a habit to dust the table once a week. This will encourage you to keep the table clutter-free.

Organizing a Basic Home Bar

Time required: 1 hour

Tending bar at home should be a pleasure, and a tidy, well-organized bar area in the dining room makes for easy entertaining. Before embarking on this project, consider any storage accessories you might want to add to your liquor cabinet or bar area, like a wine rack or a lazy Susan. Keep in mind that a bar area ideally comprises a liquor cabinet, a drawer or shelf for cocktail accessories, a wine rack, a glassware cabinet, and a nearby surface for mixing drinks.

1   Tackle the liquor cabinet and the glassware cabinet separately. Transfer the contents of the liquor cabinet to a counter or table. Discard any empty or extremely old bottles.

2   Divide liquors into categories: clear liquors, brown liquors, mixers, and liqueurs. Add to your shopping list any depleted or missing items.

3   If necessary, clean the cabinet base, walls, and door. You may also want to cover the base with shelf liner.

4   Return liquors to the cabinet, keeping your categories intact and following these rules of thumb: Frequently used items should be stored toward the front of the cabinet, with lesser used items toward the back. If desired, use a lazy Susan for easy access.

Continued →

You will need all or some of the following:

Garbage bags

Shopping list and pen

Cleaning supplies

Shelf liner

Lazy Susan

Drawer dividers

Stemware rack

5   Stock your liquor cabinet, keeping like items together. Liquors together, liqueurs together, mixers together, etc.

6   Arrange tools and utensils in the drawer, using drawer dividers if desired. Some good tools to include are: a corkscrew, a paring knife, ice cube tongs, cocktail napkins, toothpicks, and a bottle opener.

7   Transfer the contents of the glassware cabinet to a counter or table. Discard any chipped or cracked glasses, and wash any dirty glasses.

8   Divide clean glasses into categories: old-fashioned, double old-fashioned, white wine, red wine, shots, cordial, and Champagne. Add to your shopping list any items you need to replace.

9   If necessary, clean the cabinet shelves, walls, and door. You may also want to cover the shelves with liners.

10 Return the glasses to the cabinet, again keeping your categories intact and storing frequently used items toward the front of the cabinet and lesser used items toward the back. If desired, install a stemware rack on the top of the cabinet and hang your stemware upside down.

Maintenance Strategies

• After mixing a drink, or after a party, put liquors and glasses back in the areas and with the categories where they belong.

• Inventory your liquor cabinet before shopping for a holiday or special event. Put any necessary items on your shopping list.

The Dining Room

tips

A basic home bar might include some or all of the following liquors: vodka, gin, rum, Scotch, bourbon, tequila, brandy, vermouth (both sweet and dry), bitters, and Triple Sec (or Cointreau). Good accessories to have in the bar area include: a cocktail shaker, cocktail spoon, corkscrew, bottle opener, paring knife, juice squeezer, cocktail napkins, toothpicks, a small cutting board, and a bartender's guide.

ORGANIZING *Accessories*

Corner armoire. This unit fits neatly into a corner and takes up less space than an armoire set against a wall.

Fabric-lined cutlery trays, silverware drawer organizers. The compartments of good quality cutlery trays are lined with felt, velvet, or another fabric to protect silverware.

Linen-storage tissue and boxes. Table linens stored in these boxes won't get yellow or faded. Acid-free tissue paper further helps prevent yellowing.

Portable drawer storage unit. A rolling drawer unit can be used for extra storage, and can be moved out of the way when not in use. They are made from assorted materials, from plastic to metal, and available in assorted sizes and types.

Quilted china-storage containers. Available in a variety of sizes to hold plates, bowls, saucers, cups, and stemware, the containers are well padded to protect china. The containers have zippered tops, so the contents remain dust free.

Stemware rack. This rack is installed underneath an interior cabinet shelf. Stemmed glassware hangs upside down from the rack, leaving room underneath for additional storage.

Wine rack. Available in a variety of styles, sizes, and materials. Plastic or chrome, free-standing or countertop models, wine racks are a must have for those who like having a selection on hand.

the *the* **LIVING ROOM**

Perhaps you call it the living room, or the family room, or the den. Maybe you have more than one of these rooms that serve as gathering places for your family or for entertaining.

Ideally, these rooms should be comfortable and inviting, and have ample space for relaxing with family and friends. The primary challenge is to keep everything in your living room organized and conveniently located, yet also out of the way. Because aesthetics is a priority, storage should be both attractive and practical.

If you feel that your living room could function better and be more welcoming, answer the questionnaire on page 68 to help evaluate problems that need solving. You may want to get started immediately by attacking a problem area that can easily be improved. If so, turn to the simple projects on pages 78 and 82.

Living Room

questionnaire   * * *

1   **Do you avoid entertaining in your living room because it is too cluttered?**

2   **Is the room hard to clean because it has too many knickknacks, books, toys, games, and other objects?**

3   **Do you have just the necessities in your living room but not enough places to put them all?**

If you answered yes to any of these questions, your living room lacks sufficient storage. Go to page 71 for a range of tips that will help you create extra storage.

4   **Are your living room shelves and cabinets filled with books, tapes, and CDs, but are you often unable to find the book you want to read, the tape your kids want to watch, or the CD you want to play for company?**

5   **Do you have collections that seem to take up too much space?**

6   **Are you an avid reader who likes to keep past issues of magazines and journals but feels overwhelmed by the stacks interspersed throughout your living room?**

If you responded yes to any of these questions, you need to find a better way to organize your possessions and collections. For effective solutions, turn to page 73.

7   **Do family members and guests nearly trip over one another when you entertain in your living room?**

8   **Do you have difficulty having an intimate conversation with a family member or friend while comfortably seated in your living room?**

If you answered yes to either of these questions, your living room may not have the best flow. The suggestions on page 77 will help you make your living room function better for all uses.

Common Living Room Problems

Now that you have established which areas in your living room need attention, it's time to focus on solutions. Some of following ideas are sure to work for you. You will want to experiment with various solutions—and different storage accessories (page 85)—to find the best choices for your room.

Purchasing furniture is the easiest way to increase your storage immediately, if your budget permits. Various entertainment centers and furniture pieces like armoires can hold TV, video player, and stereo equipment, plus CDs and DVDs. Many units are tall and have numerous shelves and cabinets. You might also look around your living room to see where you can add other storage furniture without making the room overcrowded or impairing traffic flow.

Before you acquire any new furniture or organizing accessories (page 85), however, inventory the contents of your living room, from books and CDs to furniture like chairs and end tables. If there is an item in your living room that you don't need, find a better home for it in another room. This may be the time to dispose of old magazines you finished long ago, videotapes you never watch, games the kids no longer play, or even decorative items that do not suit the space.

tips	Try to display only one collection in your living room. Showcasing a collection of photographs, another of shells, and yet another of antique figurines will make the room look cluttered. Rather than box and store an extra collection, find another room where the objects will be shown to better advantage.

Organizing Solutions

• Add or replace furniture. You might be able to fit low shelves under a window, for storing books and especially for keeping toys, games, and other items you want to be accessible to young children. A long, narrow table placed behind the sofa can display objects from a special collection or hold a stack of books. If you have a traditional coffee table or end table, you can swap it for a chest with ample room inside or a table with drawers or shelves. This will increase available storage without taking up additional floor space.

• Go low. Flat, plastic storage boxes, practical for holding games and toys, can be slipped under many sofas. Magazines can go in baskets set under end tables, or large-format books can be stacked underneath the tables. Slip a flat, long wicker basket under the coffee table as an attractive home for neatly folded blankets and extra pillows.

• Cover up. If you don't like the busy look of baskets or stacks under a table, cover the table with decorative fabric long enough to reach the floor. Such hidden storage allows you to conceal anything you'd prefer to keep out of sight, even a sewing basket or a box of Christmas ornaments.

• Fill corners. A corner shelving unit or armoire makes efficient use of out-of-the-way spaces. Or you can fit a CD tower, a tall basket for blankets and extra cushions, or a bin for games and puzzles into an unused corner of the living room.

• Reduce bulk. Large CD and DVD collections are big space guzzlers. If you have an abundance of discs, consider discarding their jewel cases and alphabetizing them in a CD/DVD folder with protective sleeves.

• Go to the wall. Empty wall space is prime real estate, especially for collectors to display their prized ceramic plates, antique toys, or photographs. All you need is the appropriate shelving for three-dimensional objects, or frames and hanging equipment for photographs. This frees up table and shelf space.

My living room has plenty of storage space, but it is always in disarray.

Having plenty of storage space doesn't guarantee a tidy living room. On the following page are some ideas that will make it easier for you and other family members to keep things in their place. Peruse the list of accessories on page 85. Some of them will help you control the clutter.

Organizing Solutions:

Define the room. Perhaps your family uses the living room for multiple purposes—but is this desirable? Eating and drinking in the living room may result in dirty cups and plates littering the surfaces. If you pay bills and answer mail on the coffee table, you are likely to leave piles of paper-work behind. Decide with your family which activities you want to take place in the living room and come to an understanding that other activities need to be moved elsewhere.

Consolidate appliances. One way to make your living room look tidier is to put all of your electronic equipment—TV, stereo, DVD player—in a large cabinet with doors that close, such as an entertainment center. Look for one that will hold all of your equipment and accommodate your collection of discs and cassettes.

Store at arm's reach. As much as you can, keep accessories near the place where they will be used. Videotapes and DVDs should be in or near the entertainment center or other piece of furniture that holds your VCR, DVD player, and TV. Magazines and books belong near the room's reading chairs and lights, fireplace accessories on the hearth, and games near the table where they are played. The items will be easier for family members to find— and easier for them to put away.

Organize for efficiency. Often-used items should be conveniently accessible. Avoid piling your CDs on top of one another, making it hard to pull out one from the stack. Storing them in a rack, tower, or other holder will allow you to place them spine out for easy visibility and make them easy to return to the same spot. Books you refer to regularly should be on reachable shelves, whereas photo albums and collectibles belong on high shelves.

Gang knickknacks. A living room can look cluttered if small standing frames, miniatures, or other small items are scattered throughout the room on tables and shelves. Your collection will look more organized if grouped in one location: pictures on one wall, miniatures on one shelf.

Displaying your collections

Some collections end up in boxes, hogging storage space and hidden from sight. Whatever you collect, be it carnival glass or Bakelite jewelry, you may want to consider creating a dedicated display space in your living room, where you can enjoy your treasures every day. Here are a few solutions that may help you coax your collection out of its hiding place.

- If it's flat, frame it. Maps, vintage postcards, or quilt squares can be protected in frames and hung on the wall. Gang small items like found photographs into one large frame for an interesting collage effect.

- Small three-dimensional items such as souvenir spoons, fountain pens, or bottlecaps can also be hung on the wall even if they won't fit in standard picture frames. Shadow boxes are frames with a generous depth for showcasing items that aren't flat.

- An old pie safe, a china cabinet, or a bookshelf can be converted into a display cabinet for anything from collectible glass and tableware to china teacups or tin toys. Look for a cabinet with glass doors to protect items from dust and inquisitive fingers.

- For popular collectibles, such as coins or stamps, you can easily find custom-designed displays, from tabletop to wall mounted.

My living room doesn't seem to flow and feels awkward when I entertain family and friends.

This is a very common problem. Your living room may be perfectly comfortable when you're in it alone, but as soon as you have a few people over, the seating arrangements inhibit conversation or block traffic flow. Here are some simple reorganizing ideas to make your living room a more convivial place.

| tips | If it hasn't happened to you yet, it soon will. You reach for a remote to change the TV channel, but find only the remote for the DVD player. No doubt, your living room is like those in many homes—filled with a complete array of entertainment equipment, including TV, CD player, tape deck, and DVD player. If you invest in a universal remote that operates all equipment, you won't have various remotes scattered about the room, and control of all electronic devices will be at your fingertips. |

Organizing Solutions:

- **Forge a path.** Keep in mind that you and your guests should be able to navigate the room easily and reach all seats without turning sideways to squeeze between pieces of furniture.

- **Provide gathering places.** Family members and guests need to be able to sit near one another so they can talk without raising their voices. Arrange your sofa and chairs into conversational groupings and be sure that there are enough surfaces for beverages.

- **Choose furniture with multiple uses.** An ottoman can double as a side table or coffee table. A small bookshelf can store books and be a surface for a lamp and beverages. A chest can double as a coffee table and can store games.

- **Think beyond the outlet.** Most people install electronic equipment wherever an outlet is located, but especially in older homes, outlets can be in inconvenient places. Rather than being limited by the existing sites of electrical outlets, consider hiring an electrician to install outlets in better locations. Another obvious option is to use extension cords. Consider covering extension cords with specially made covers or channels that look like part of the baseboard molding.

Organizing Your Photographs

Time required: 3–5 hours

Photographs are forever, especially if they are properly cared for. Organizing your photographs will allow you to enjoy them and also to share them with others. The added benefit is that a well-organized photo collection will take up less space. Before you start, decide how you want to store the pictures—in albums or photo boxes—or if you have the space to display frames, then purchase the necessary accessories.

1   Gather all your photographs in one place. If you have too many loose photographs to organize in one sitting, choose a particular theme, such as holiday parties or your last five years of camping trips or your various family reunions.

2   Decide how you want to organize and categorize your photos. Chronological order is the obvious choice, but you might prefer another approach, say, by family member or location. Designate a shoe box for each category and label it.

3   Divide the photos and their corresponding negatives into categories, and place in the boxes. Discard any photos that you don't like and will never display, and duplicates that you don't need. Put duplicates you intend to give away in an outgoing mail pile. Stack the photos you want to frame in a separate pile.

You will need all or some of the following:

Large shoe boxes or similar containers

Felt-tip pen

Garbage bag

Photo albums, photo boxes, and/or picture frames

4   Beginning with one of the boxes, review the photos again, to make sure that all are worth keeping. Arrange the photos in a photo album or place in a photo box, and frame any pictures you've designated for framing. Date the negatives and file them in a separate box. Place the photo boxes on or under a living room table, the albums on a shelf, and the frames on the wall, tables, or shelves.

Maintenance Strategies

Before developing film, make sure you already have a place to store the photographs. Or, when you pick up your developed pictures, purchase a new album, an empty photo box, or new frames.

Right after bringing the photos home, go through them and toss those you do not want to keep. Date the back of each picture using a special pen designed for this purpose. Immediately put your photos into an album or box. Date and file the negatives, placing them in the location where you store all your negatives.

If you ordered duplicates for a friend or family member, mail them immediately so they won't be overlooked.

tips   With a digital camera you can easily organize your photos on your computer. Photos can then be stored on CD or DVD, and sent by e-mail.

tips

Instead of spending a lot of money on frames—which you may not have shelf or wall space to display—hang a bulletin board or a magnet board for showing off your snapshots. You can easily make changes and additions as you develop each new roll of film.

Organizing Your CD Collection

Time required: 1–2 hours

Although they are smaller than records, CDs add up. If you don't have a good place to store them, they spill off shelves and clutter up drawers, and it can be frustratingly hard to find a recording you want to hear.

Before you start, you'll want to decide on the type and size of the storage that you prefer—or which best suits your living room. CD caddies that hold fifty or a hundred discs are compact because you don't need the jewel cases. Towers and shelves also work well for CDs. Most of these units require that CDs be in cases. Whichever storage solution you prefer, allow room for your collection to grow. This project can also be done for DVDs, videos, and video games.

1   Gather all your CDs. Remember to collect any you have stashed in your car.

2   Decide on a system of organization, whether by genre of music or alphabetical by recording artist. Then sort the CDs by the categories you've chosen. As you do this, make a pile of unwanted CDs to give away or resell. Discard scratched or damaged CDs.

3   If you are keeping your CDs in jewel cases, assess the condition of the cases. Discard any broken cases, and transfer the CDs and printed matter to a new case.

4   Keeping the CDs organized according to categories, install them in your chosen storage units and place the units in the living room.

You will need all or some of the following:

Garbage bag

Empty jewel cases

CD caddies, towers, shelves, or racks

Maintenance Strategies

As for the day-to-day maintenance, there's no secret formula here. If you put each CD back in its proper place, you'll be able to find it the next time.

For the long term, try going through your CDs twice a year, getting rid of those CDs you have outgrown or no longer enjoy. Many record stores that deal in both new and used CDs offer a cash or trade-in value for your used discs.

ORGANIZING *Accessories*

- **Baskets.** Like shelves, baskets are versatile. They can hold pillows, magazines, books, toys—just about anything that you want to have on hand but need to keep contained and out of the way.

- **CD caddies, racks, and towers.** There are myriad options for CD storage. Some units can hold more than a hundred CDs. Others are small and fit on a shelf. Similar units are available for audiotapes, DVDs, and video-tapes.

- **Flat, plastic storage boxes.** Ideal for slipping under sofas, these low-profile storage containers can be used to store photos, games, extra blankets and throw pillows, or videos.

- **Frames.** The variety is infinite—frames for hanging on the wall, frames for displaying on a shelf, even large frames that accommodate multiple pictures.

- **Magazine racks.** Many racks take up little space and can be set next to a reading light and end table, making them unobtrusive.

- **Magazine-storage boxes.** These acrylic boxes are best for storing magazines that you are saving for reference. They keep the magazines upright and allow you to see the spines, and also fit neatly on bookshelves.

- **Photo albums and photo-storage boxes.** If you take lots of photographs, albums and boxes are the best way to store them, especially if you do not have adequate space to display framed pictures. Many boxes are suitable for display on a shelf or table and have a lid that functions as a frame for a single photograph. Be sure to purchase archival-quality albums and boxes, which will not damage your photos during long-term storage.

- **Shelves.** These are among the most indispensable tools for creating an organized room. Shelves come in almost every dimension and configuration imaginable: tall and narrow, short and wide; shaped to fit in corners or designed to be freestanding in the middle of a room. Some units can be outfitted with doors that hide some of the shelves, thereby creating an inexpensive cabinet.

the **HOME OFFICE**

Chapter 4

For many people, having a home office is as important as having a dining room or a living room.

Even if the home office is not used as your primary workplace or as an adjunct to your place of employment, it is the location where you conduct the business of running your home—paying bills and storing important documents like insurance policies. This may also be the place where a computer is installed for everyone in your household to surf the Internet and answer e-mail.

Dedicating a separate room or a section of an existing room to a home office will help you organize your busy life and that of other household members. The space should be big enough to allow you to pay bills, sort and answer mail, file paperwork, and use your computer. This chapter covers many options for setting up and organizing a home office. Every office, however, needs some basic elements: a desk, chair, phone, computer, filing cabinet, bookcase or shelves, organizing containers, and assorted office supplies.

Whether you already have a home office or need to set up one, answer the questionnaire on page 90 to determine your needs and where you should begin.

Home Office
questionnaire ✳ ✳ ✳

1   **Do you use your dining room or kitchen table or your living room coffee table as your home office?**

2   **Are piles of bills, lists, and mail kept in several locations scattered about the house?**

3   **Are the supplies you need—stamps, envelopes, pens, extra checks, medical records—stored in different locations?**

If you have answered yes to any of these questions, you need to set up a home office in a dedicated space. Turn to page 93 to choose the best space to use and to learn how to establish an office.

4   **Do you sometimes pay bills late because you don't have a way to keep track of due bills in your home office?**

5   **Do you get frustrated when looking for an important piece of paper or other item in your office because it's not where it should be?**

If yes is the answer to either question, the desk and storage in your office are in disarray and your paperwork may be out of control. Go to page 95 for solutions to this problem common to many households.

Common Home Office Problems

Now that you know the areas in your home office that need attention—or if the very lack of an office in your home is causing your problems—you can start to focus on solutions. You will want to experiment with various organizing suggestions—and different accessories (page 106)—to find the best choices for your home office. If you already have a home office and need to get control of the ever-mounting piles of paperwork, in the following pages you will find two simple projects that you can do immedlately to make a better-functioning office.

The first step is choosing a space that will work best for you and others in your household. An office can be incorporated into just about any part of the house, if you do not have a spare room that can be converted for the purpose. It is important that your office be in a low-traffic area and that you have access to an electrical outlet. An entryway, the kitchen, and hallways generally should be avoided, unless the portion devoted to an office is spacious enough to allow you to work uninterrupted. Better choices might be a niche under a staircase or an out-of-the-way corner of a bedroom or living room that can accommodate a desk and other necessities, such as a file cabinet. You can use one of many attractive folding screens on the market to close off the office from the rest of the room.

If space is tight in your home, you may need to think creatively. Perhaps you have a closet that can be emptied and made into an office with a desk, wall-mounted shelves, and a canvas shoe caddy inside the door for holding supplies. You can work with the door open, then close the door on the office when you're done.

Above all, it is important to analyze your work habits before choosing a location for your office and outfitting it with furniture and accessories. If you like to spread out materials, you will need a large surface area. On the other hand, if you rely on a computer for much of your work—even for paying your bills and managing your checkbook—a smaller surface may suffice, as long as you have sufficient space for computer peripherals such as a printer.

Dedicate a work surface. Depending on the location of your office, you want a desk that is large enough for all your activities—and won't be used for other purposes. You don't need to purchase the latest trendy, most expensive piece of furniture. A piece of plywood—cut to fit, then sanded and painted or stained—set across two filing cabinets makes an inexpensive and practical desk. This arrangement automatically gives you two cabinets close at hand for filing paperwork. If even a standard desk is unfeasible, a small table or a pull-down shelf is a good substitute. If you use a computer, the desk should be able to accommodate it and still give you enough surface area for writing and filing.

Allow sufficient filing space. Although futurists once predicted that we would work in so-called paperless offices, the paperwork in most people's lives mounts up fast. The only solution is to make sure that you have enough filing and drawer space. If you do not have a desk with file cabinets or your desk storage is limited, you can use rolling file cabinets. These units, often made of wood, can be tucked under a table or in a closet when not in use. The top of the file cabinet can provide supplementary work space. Metal file boxes and rolling file carts can be handy as well, especially if you don't have much paperwork to store and you don't have room for standard file cabinets.

Pull up a chair. The importance of having a comfortable chair cannot be overstated. If you don't like sitting in your chair, you may be tempted to pick up your work and move it to another room of the house, spreading clutter where it is not welcome. Having the right chair is also important to your well-being. The height of the seat, and even the armrests and back, should be adjustable so you can work free of strain and stress at your computer keyboard or on a flat surface. You also may need an adjustable chair if other family members will be using the office.

Go to the wall. A bulletin board is a great space saver and allows you to display important information without cluttering your desk surface. You can post daily reminders, bills and receipts, important phone numbers, and to-do lists. You can also use a host of other wall-mounted organizers and accessories, from in/out baskets and mail sorters to calendars.

Don't underestimate ambience. Without going into a home-decorating frenzy, you can make your office comfortable and inviting. If it has good lighting, along with a practical desk, a suitable chair for desk and computer work, and adequate filing space, you're more likely to use the space, get your work done, and keep your office organized. Without cluttering your office, you can enhance the ambience by adding personal touches such as framed family photos or artwork.

My desk is in disarray, and I can seldom find what I need.

Many people feel that they need to keep important paperwork like bills on a visible surface. The rationale is understandable: if it can't be seen, it doesn't exist. As bills, mail, and receipts pile up, however, the desk surface disappears, burying not only your bills and mail but also pens, date book, and other necessities. You can still store papers where they are accessible without creating clutter by following the suggestions on the following page. If you need to set up a file system or mail system, you'll want to do one of the projects beginning on page 100.

Organizing your office and setting up systems that work for you are only the first steps to achieving a functional office. Make a rule that at the end of each day, the goal is to clear off your desk— by putting papers in your in/out baskets or filing them in your file cabinet. Or you can establish a "hot" file of items that need your immediate attention the following morning.

tips

Whether you are establishing a home office or reorganizing an existing office, you need to protect important paperwork. Fireproof safes can be used to store documents, backup computer disks, and valuable items such as heirloom jewelry. These small safes can fit under a desk or in the corner of a closet. Extremely important documents, such as social security cards, birth certificates, marriage license, insurance policies, stock and bond certificates, wills, mortgage and loan papers, and real-estate deeds, should be kept in a bank safe-deposit box. You can photocopy these documents and keep the copies in a home safe or other location.

Organize by category and for efficiency. Put your office supplies where they are easy to locate and keep like items together—pens, pencils, erasers, small notepads, stapler and staples, computer disks. Drawer dividers can be installed to hold the various categories so you can always find them. If you do not have a desk or table with drawers, store supplies by category in stacking baskets or clear plastic containers. Containers designed especially for computer disks protect the disks from dust. Some disk organizers have dividers that let you sort the disks by category. Any item that you need frequently should be close at hand. If you work more often on the computer than on paper, you will want to have your computer disks nearby but store notepads on a shelf, in a bottom drawer, or in the back of a file cabinet.

Use in/out baskets. Papers that need to be signed, notices of changes of address or phone number, and other papers that need immediate attention should be put in your in basket as soon as you open the mail. Out baskets are for outgoing mail or papers to be filed. In/out baskets come in many forms: stacking baskets that sit on your desk or wall-mounted baskets that free up the desk surface. You can also use a container that is divided into two spacious pockets and holds papers vertically rather than horizontally.

Set up a file system. No matter how much paperwork piles up in your household, it can be controlled with a good file system. Refer to the project on page 100 for establishing a file system and to the sidebars on pages 98 and 102 for deciding what to keep and what to discard and how to categorize your paperwork before filing it. Once you have a system in place that works for you, file documents as soon as possible, whether a new insurance policy, a just-paid bill, or your child's report card. If possible, keep the filing cabinet within arm's reach of your desk to encourage prompt filing.

Go digital. You can minimize paper by doing some of your work online. Your address book can be stored on your computer (make sure you keep a backup disk in a safe place). You can also pay bills online and keep to-do lists and tax records on your computer.

Continued →

• **Consolidate notes and lists.** Avoid writing notes and lists on small pieces of paper, which can get lost and are difficult to organize. Instead, use a single spiral-bound notebook or steno pad. You can attach labeled tabs to the pages so you can easily find each category of list. If you use multiple calendars—say, a handheld computer, a date book, and a wall or desk calendar—settle on one primary calendar with a format that can accommodate all your appointments. Even address books can get disorganized. Maybe the pages of yours are filled and are also interleaved with business cards and pieces of paper bearing handwritten names and addresses. Consider using a card file or other system that gives your address records room to grow and allows you to discard names and addresses that are no longer current.

• **Go to the wall.** If you have wall space, install a bulletin board for displaying invitations, event tickets, phone lists, and other information that you want to have visible but don't want cluttering the top of your desk.

• **Control wires.** Install a power strip under your desk to accommodate all of your office equipment, such as cordless phone, computer, printer, scanner, and fax machine. Use twist-ties to gather and hold the excess wire in neat bundles, and label cords with color-coded stickers for easy identification.

• **Avoid excess paper.** Think before you order a magazine, taking time to decide if you really need every issue. Would a better choice be to read it at the library or borrow past issues from a friend? Rather than request catalogs and brochures, go online to peruse the offerings and services. Don't download and print information from the Internet every time you look something up. Instead, add the Web site to your Internet file or bookmarks so you can easily refer to it again.

tips

If you don't already have a computer and intend to purchase one for your home office, consider a laptop, which is ideal for a small office or a desk with limited space. When not in use, it can be folded up and stored out of sight. If you need a full-size computer or are contemplating an upgrade, you may want to purchase one with a flat-screen monitor, which will save up to 12 inches of space.

To toss, or not to toss?

Before you set up a filing system—or if you are cleaning out existing files—you need to decide what to keep and what to discard. You'll also want to identify any documents that can be put in deep storage or should be kept in a safe-deposit box. If you have extensive files or you are placing files in deep storage, create a directory, or list of files, so you know where everything is located.

Important papers that you must keep:

- Birth and death certificates

- Health records

- Insurance policies such as life, homeowner's, and auto

- Marriage, divorce, custody, and adoption papers and certificates

- Mortgage and loan papers (keep for three years after the loan is paid off)

- Passports

- Property deeds

- Receipts and warranties for appliances and other items you currently own

- Stock and bond certificates

- Tax records (business records for at least seven years, personal for four years; if in doubt about your situation, consult your tax accountant)

- Wills

Papers you can discard or recycle:

- Articles or brochures you haven't read or referred to in several years

- ATM and deposit slips after you record them in your checkbook and reconcile your monthly bank statement

- Bank and credit-card statements more than one year old unless you itemize your tax deductions

- Business cards you no longer need

- Expired coupons

- Old grocery receipts

- Papers relating to expired insurance policies

- Pay stubs at the end of the calendar year and after you have reconciled them with your tax documents

- Receipts and warranties for items you no longer own

- Receipts for regular bills, such as phone and utility, that are not tax deductible (keep bills for the current month until the next ones arrive)

Setting Up a File System

Time required: 2–3 hours

If you don't already have file cabinets, you'll want to select the system that will work best for your office. Vertical files are conventional cabinets that store file folders front to back. These files take up less floor space than lateral files but are usually taller. Lateral files are wider than they are deep; they are usually not as tall as vertical files and generally take up more floor space. The advantage of lateral files is that the files run side to side, giving you easy access to the full row of file folders.

You will also need to choose from two basic types of file folders: conventional manila folders that sit in file drawers, or hanging files suspended from a metal rack that fits inside the file drawer. You can label manila folders by writing on the tabs. Hanging folders come with file tabs that are inserted in the slots provided along the edge of each folder.

1   Gather all the loose papers in your office, as well as any documents, receipts, and the like scattered elsewhere in the house. Now that you have everything spread out, you need to decide what to keep and what to discard. Referring to the lists on page 98, throw out or recycle what you don't need. If you can't decide about a particular document, put it aside and review it after you are finished. Whether or not you should keep it may be clear later. If you are discarding any papers that contain personal information such as social security numbers or numbers of bank accounts, be sure to shred them. If there is something you need to deal with immediately, put it in your in basket or establish a "hot" folder.

You will need:

Garbage bag

Filing cabinet(s)

File folders and labels or file tabs

Permanent markers, in various colors if desired

2   Sort your paperwork into file categories, referring
     to the list on page 102. Many of these categories
     may apply to you. You may need to establish
     others relevant to your household. The list is
     arranged by major categories, each of which is
     followed by subcategories. When you've finished
     sorting, you should have a pile for each category
     or subcategory. Then you can arrange each pile
     chronologically, with the most recent item on top.
     If you are storing last year's tax receipts and tax
     returns in your file cabinet—or other important
     papers that you do not need to refer to regularly—
     box the files and store them in a storage closet or
     in your attic or basement.

3   Label the file folders, using a system that will
     work for your categories, then put the papers in
     their corresponding folders. If you are using hang-
     ing folders, these can be labeled with the major
     categories. Inside each hanging folder, you can slip
     a manila folder labeled with each subcategory.
     For instance, you may have a hanging file labeled
     "bank"; the manila folders inside it might be for
     "car loan" and "household checking account."
     But if you have too many subcategories to fit in
     one hanging folder or you are using manila folders
     alone, you can devote one file per category or
     subcategory. Another system that might work for
     you is using a different color marker to label the
     files in each category: blue for all the utility folders,
     red for each credit card, for instance.

4   Arrange your files in the file cabinet(s). You want
     to keep the files you need most frequently near
     the front of each drawer or where you can reach
     them easily. If your files are extensive and you
     have placed some of them in another location, you
     should consider making a directory—a list of files
     by category—so you know where each one is.

Maintenance Strategies

Presort papers by placing them in
file folders with headings such as
"pass on," "recycle," "sign and send."
These folders can be kept in your
in/out baskets.

Always put files and papers back
where they belong as soon as possible
after using them.

File regularly so piles of paperwork
do not build up. If you can't file
papers every day, use an in box or
folder to store papers until you have
time to file them.

If you receive a notice for a change
of address or new phone number or
an announcement of an upcoming
event, act on it immediately. Add the
new information to your computer
address book, Rolodex file, date
book, or master calendar. Then throw
the notice away.

Clean out your files once a year.
Decide what you can discard. Put files
you need to keep—such as last year's
tax records and filings—into a file
box, label it, and store it in an out-
of-the-way place such as a storage
closet or your basement or attic. If
you keep a directory of files, add the
name of the box and a description of
its contents.

What goes where?

The categories below are the ones you're likely to need in your home-filing system. The main categories are followed by subcategories. When you set up your system, you'll need to decide the categories that will work best for you.

- Appliances: one file per appliance for warranties, instruction manuals, lists of authorized service centers

- Automobile: one file per vehicle

- Bank: checking, savings, IRA, loans

- Brokerage accounts: one file per account

- Children's files: one file for each child with school records, sports information, class lists

- Correspondence: choose subcategories that apply to your household

- Credit/cash: one file per credit card, plus a file for general cash receipts (receipts with tax implications go in a tax file)

- Employment: résumés, employee-benefits information, pension records

- Financial planning: budgets, financial plans

- Insurance: separate files for homeowners, auto, and liability policies (photocopy the policies and keep the originals in a safe-deposit box or other off-site location)

- Life documents: birth certificates, passports, marriage license, life-insurance policies, stock and bond certificates, wills, mortgage and loan papers, property deeds (photocopy all documents and keep the originals in a safe-deposit box or other off-site location)

- Medical: doctors' names, addresses, and phone numbers; forms; and medical plan handbooks; one file for each family member or provider

- Personal files: topics of personal interest to you such as books to read or information on nutrition

- Personal property inventory: records including original price of valuable items, model and serial numbers, and photos of possessions (a photocopy of the inventory belongs in your safe-deposit box)

- Tax records: one or more files for receipts and other documents needed to file the current year's state and federal taxes

- Utilities: gas and electric, telephone, cable TV, trash pickup

- Vacation: places you would like to visit, places you've been to, clippings about restaurants and hotels

Some computer scanners are designed specifically for scanning business cards. If you have many cards that you need to keep, consider purchasing one of these scanners and the appropriate software so you can add the cards to your computer files rather than keeping them loose in a drawer or on your desk.

Setting Up a Mail System

Time required: 1–2 hours

Paperwork often starts to get disorganized as soon as it enters the house. If you set up a system for outgoing mail—and for answering the mail—you'll get a jump on the clutter. This project repurposes a hanging canvas shoe caddy, turning it into a great mail sorting system for the entire family. If you haven't the wall space, desktop vertical file sorters or stacking trays can stand in.

1   Clear an area on the wall in or near your home office. Hang the shoe caddy and put the trash basket nearby.

2   Designate one pocket for each member of the family. You may also want to dedicate pockets to various categories, such as bills to pay, correspondence to answer, letters to mail, and invitations. Label a card for each person and category and staple it to a pocket.

3   Use the remaining pockets to hold pens, envelopes, and other mailing supplies. Label these pockets as well.

4   When the mail arrives, distribute it to the various family members. Place urgent mail, such as bills to pay, in your in basket. Recycle the empty envelopes along with any junk mail. Designate holders or baskets for magazines or catalogs, rather than piling them on your office desk or in other parts of the house.

You will need all or some of the following:

Small hanging canvas shoe caddy

Trash basket

Small blank business-sized cards

Felt-tip pen

Stapler

Pens, envelopes, stamps, address labels, and other mailing supplies

Magazine holders or baskets

Maintenance Strategies

Go through your mail every day and distribute it according to the system you've established. If your mail arrives and you won't be sorting it until later in the day, always put it in a designated place near your mail system or in your home office so you don't have to search for it later.

When bills come in, write on the outside of the return envelope the date that the payment needs to be mailed. Then, put the bills in a dedicated folder or in basket, post them on a bulletin board, or place them in another area where you won't overlook them.

Get rid of junk mail immediately, as well as items that do not interest you. Be sure to shred all pre-approved credit-card applications and mail that includes your social security information or your credit-card numbers.

Buy a personalized return-address stamp with a built-in inkpad. Use this rather than writing your return address on every envelope. Keep the stamp with your other mailing supplies.

To manage the influx of catalogs, discard old catalogs when new ones arrive. When you decide to purchase an item, tear out the page showing the item and the order form, then toss the catalog. If you receive unwanted catalogs, write or phone the company and request that your name and address be removed from the mailing list.

tips	Most banks offer online banking. The service is usually provided for a nominal fee, and no special software is required. There are many benefits to online banking: no check writing, no mailing, no stamps. You can do your banking from home or even on your lunch break at work.

The following readily available organizing accessories are relatively inexpensive and can be found in housewares stores and home improvement and office supply stores and catalogs.

Accordion file folders. These folders have multiple dividers; some include a pocket for each letter of the alphabet. You can use them to organize your correspondence or tax records, or keep magazine and newspaper clippings.

Bulletin board. This great space saver allows you to display important information such as daily reminders, important phone numbers, and school schedules.

Cable ties, clips, and organizers. Get your cords in order with specially made accessories. From simple twist-ties and wall-mounted clips to spools that keep cords wound neatly beneath a flexible shell, there are many accessories that can help you control cords.

Computer cart. If you haven't enough space on your desk to hold your computer and all its peripherals, a computer cart can be the solution. These come in different sizes, and are made from various materials from wood to metal. Look for one with wheels, which will enable you to roll your entire system out of sight when company comes.

Desk organizers. The array of these desk-top containers is limitless: cups to hold pencils and pens, trays for letters, sorters for mail, telephone holders with a space underneath for a notepad and pen. Some products, such as lazy Susans for the desktop, have multiple organizers all in one unit. You might also consider specialized organizers for computer disks and CDs.

Dry erase/chalkboard. If you have a busy household and plenty of wall space, use a chalkboard to leave messages for family members and post important phone numbers.

File cabinets. You have many choices: legal and standard size, vertical files and lateral files. Some cabinets have frames that hold hanging folders rather than standard manila folders.

Hanging canvas shoe caddy. Using a caddy on a wall or on the back of a closet door is an easy way to set up a mail system (see page 104), hold bills and correspondence, or store office supplies.

In/out baskets. These baskets are essential for prioritizing your paperwork. You can find interlocking units that allow you to stack as many baskets as you need. Some are made of wire, others of plastic.

Keyboard tray. This shallow tray maximizes desktop space by taking the keyboard off the desk surface and fitting it beneath your desk, above your knees. It slides out for work, and back under your desk when not in use.

Magazine holders. Made of cardboard or clear acrylic plastic, these holders store magazines upright so you can see the spines. If you subscribe to many publications, you may also want to designate a special bin or basket where you stow new arrivals after sorting the mail.

Rolling file cabinets, rolling file carts, and file boxes. Rolling cabinets and carts that hold files can be slipped under a desk or table or into a closet and brought out only when needed. Metal and plastic file boxes can likewise be stored out of the way if your office cannot accommodate conventional file cabinets. Paperwork going into deep storage can be put in cardboard file boxes.

Rolodex files. Some files sit flat on the desk. Others hang from a frame and store address cards in the round. Cards can be discarded if an address is no longer current, and new names and addresses can be added, avoiding the clutter that can accumulate in an address book.

Stacking bins and drawers. Use stacking units to store computer paper and other office supplies, especially if your desk lacks sufficient drawer space. Plastic containers are useful because you can see the contents. They can be stashed out of sight so your floor space is not cluttered.

Wall organizers. If you have a small desk, you'll want to consider using the wall to organize office supplies and other necessities. One option is wall pockets, which mount in a vertical line like shelves and can be linked together. You can also find wall-mounted in/out baskets and other organizers—or you can install a shelf to hold desk organizers that will not fit on your work surface.

the **BEDROOM**

The bedroom is a sanctuary, the place where you retreat after a long, hard day. Of all the rooms in your home, this one should be the most free of distractions.

But with clothing draped over your bed, dresser, and nightstand; shoes scattered about the floor; and dirty laundry piled in a corner, the bedroom can accumulate its share of clutter. Primary storage areas in the bedroom are the closet and dresser drawers. By applying various organizational strategies, you can stretch this bedroom storage by as much as 60 percent.

The first step is determining the areas of your bedroom that need attention by answering the brief questionnaire on page 112. If you are eager to get started, you may want to try one of the simple projects beginning on page 126, which will immediately improve the organization of your bedroom.

Bedroom
questionnaire * * *

1 : **When all of your clothes are clean and hung up, is your closet bursting at the seams?**

2 : **Do you often need to layer a few blouses or pants on one hanger?**

3 : **Are your shoes piled on the floor of the closet and under your bed, making it hard to find matching pairs?**

If you answered yes to any of these questions, you may not have enough closet space. Don't despair—many homes have small bedroom closets. On page 117, you'll find tips for maximizing the space in your closet, regardless of its size.

4 : **Is it hard for you to get dressed in the morning or for a special event because you are unable to find the clothes you want to wear?**

5 : **Do you tend to wear the same shirts, pants, and skirts over and over?**

6 : **When you purchase a new item of clothing, do you later realize you already own something like it?**

A yes answer to any of these questions indicates that your closet may be in disarray. Turn to page 121 for tips that will enable you to find what you want when you need it.

7 : **Do you keep stacks of folded shirts and sweaters on the floor or in laundry baskets or bins?**

8 : **Do you use your dresser top for storing clothing you wear regularly?**

9 : **Are you having difficulty closing your dresser drawers?**

If yes is the response to any of these questions, you probably don't have enough drawer space. The solutions on page 123 will help you make better use of your dresser drawers and add storage to your bedroom.

10 : **Is it difficult for you to find what you are looking for in your drawers?**

11 : **When you remove a shirt or sweater from a drawer, is it too wrinkled to wear?**

12 : **Does each drawer contain a jumble of clothes and accessories such as ties, scarves, and belts?**

A yes answer to any of these questions suggests that your drawers are in disarray. On page 125, you'll find tips for reorganizing your drawers.

Common Bedroom Problems

Now that you know the areas of your bedroom that need attention, here are various solutions to consider. You'll also want to review the storage accessories on page 134 and choose those best suited to your situation. If your closet or drawers need a thorough cleaning out, the projects on the following pages will help you get started.

I don't have enough closet space.

Having a small closet is not as much of a liability as you think. The interior of a small closet is easy to take in at a glance. Also, a small closet forces you to keep your clothes organized. Even a large closet is easy to fill to capacity.

If your closet is as organized as it can be and you are still short of space, you may need to purchase an armoire for your bedroom, providing the room can accommodate it without impeding traffic flow.

Whether or not you add storage furniture to your bedroom, the following solutions will help you find extra space in your closet. Those that will work best for you will depend on the proportions of your closet and the nature of the items you need to store in it.

Sort and discard. Periodically, you need to empty your closet and dispose of or donate clothes, shoes, and accessories you no longer wear. Unused hangers also take up space by getting tangled on your closet pole or falling onto the floor. A better place for them is in a laundry or utility room, or you can give them to your dry cleaner.

Turn to deep storage. Clothes that you wear only in certain seasons—such as heavy winter coats and sweaters, ski clothes, or summer-vacation wear—can be neatly packed in plastic bins or garment bags and kept in your attic or basement or other storage area. When you choose a location, make sure that it is free of excess moisture. Or, if you have a particularly tall or deep closet, place infrequently used clothes in bins toward the back of the closet or near the ceiling on shelves. These items can also go in large, flat plastic containers specially made to be slipped under a bed.

Adjust the closet pole. You don't have to settle for the current placement of the pole in your closet; reinstalling it may allow you to gain space to add shelves above your hanging clothes. To determine the correct height for the pole, measure the longest piece of clothing that hangs in your closet and add two inches. Allow for the depth of the hangers, plus another two or three inches in the back of the closet so hangers can slide freely along the pole without interference from the back wall. If you have a wooden pole, consider replacing it with a metal one, which allows hangers to be moved with greater ease.

Hang efficiently. Group all long, hanging items such as long coats and skirts on one section of the pole, all shirts and short hanging items in another section. From the main pole, you can hang a second, shorter pole—it will fall about three feet below the main pole, just below the short clothes—for hanging additional short items, or you can add one of the types of floor storage discussed below.

Add floor storage. Rather than using a hanging shoe caddy, you can store your shoes in clear shoe boxes, or even in their original boxes (it's helpful to label the boxes), and neatly stack them on the floor. Special shoe holders have slanted shelves that allow you to see and access the shoes easily. Alternating the shoes toe-in and toe-out on the shelves will save space. If your closet has plenty of floor space, you can also use stackable bins to hold clothing, or you can fit stacking drawers or a small dresser underneath shirts and other short clothes on hangers.

Continued →

Add shelving. If you do not already have shelves above the closet pole—and the ceiling in your closet is high enough—add a shelf a short distance above the pole for folded clothing that you wear frequently and a shelf above that for items you use less often. If shelves above the pole are unfeasible and you do not need the entire pole for hanging clothes, you can install a canvas hanging shelf unit which can hold everything from shoes and scarves to sweaters and jeans.

Call for backup. The back of your closet door can accommodate any number of organizing accessories. You can install a shoe caddy or hanging shoe shelf, enabling you to store your shoes off the floor. A caddy can also hold scarves, belts, or socks, especially if you lack drawer space in your bedroom. Racks on the closet door are great for hanging belts or ties. Hooks are also useful for casual clothing. Avoid hanging prized items on hooks; they can easily get stretched out of shape.

| tips | Everything in your closet should be easy to see. Here are a few tips for creating an inviting closet where clothes, shoes, and accessories are at your fingertips. |

- Paint your closet interior bright white. A washable semigloss paint will allow you to remove scuffs and fingerprints.

- Install fluorescent lighting and use "white" bulbs, which will enable you to see colors more accurately. The light source should be placed in the center of the ceiling and be bright enough to illuminate your entire closet. Track lighting or recessed lighting, which generates considerable heat, should be used only in room-size closets.

- Replace sliding doors. If it's difficult to see or access the depths of your closet, it's even more difficult to keep it organized. Sliding doors obscure half of your closet. Double swinging doors allow you to view the complete contents of your closet at a glance. If you only have a single closet door, consider enlarging the closet opening and then installing double doors.

The Bedroom

Room to grow

A child's bedroom is a place to rest and sleep as well as a place to study and play. A well-organized bedroom allows for all these functions, and is easier to keep tidy. Here are some organizing solutions for this hardworking room.

- Sort all the play equipment and designate an area for each—arts and crafts materials go on one shelf or in one drawer, stuffed animals in another, games in another.

- Store playthings within easy reach. If the child can reach their toys or books themselves, they are more likely to learn to put things away when they are through.

- Containerize small, loose toys. Clear plastic containers will keep a miniature toy collection in check. Look for containers with easy-to-open lids.

- Label shelves, crates, and boxes with their contents. Identifying where things go will help children put items back where they belong.

- Store clothing within reach. Open cubbies or stackable cube-shaped bins can be a good alternative to the more grown-up chest of drawers, as they make it easier for children to put the clothing away.

- Install two rods in the closet. One up high for dress clothes and off-season wear, and one within reach for everyday, in-season clothing.

- Install a shelf around the top perimeter of the walls to display beloved dolls or stuffed animals that your child no longer uses but is not prepared to give up.

- If you have more than one child, mark or label the clothes for easier sorting after laundry time.

I have plenty of closet space, but my clothes tend to be in disarray.

At some point in the week, you probably need to get dressed in a hurry before going to work or attending an event. These are the moments when a disorganized closet can be the most frustrating. There's no reason, however, that you can't have a closet that functions every time you open it. When you can find the clothing you want, you are less likely to overlook the items you own or purchase items you don't need.

Before you organize your closet, you need to empty it, sort through your clothes, and dispose of or donate items that you no longer wear or are beyond repair. You'll undoubtedly discover that unwanted clothing was taking up valuable space and adding to the disarray.

tips

The shoes you wear most frequently should be accessible—by storing them on the floor, on a shoe shelf, or in a hanging caddy. Shoes worn less often are best kept in boxes on a shelf or on the floor in the back of the closet, so they'll remain free of dust and scuffs. You can label the boxes or even attach snapshots of the shoes so you don't have to rummage through every box to find a particular pair. Before you arrange the shoes, remove those in need of polishing or repair, and put them in a designated place until you can care for them.

• **Arrange by category.** Hang each type of clothing together. Grouping shirts, pants, suits, and dresses will help you select the shirt you want to wear with a particular suit or the dress you need for a special event. Depending on the nature of your wardrobe, you can also separate casual clothes from those you wear to work, or you can color-code your hanging clothes from light to dark. Apply a similar system to folded clothing on shelves. Sort shoes by season, color, and/or type (formal, informal, athletic), then store them together in a shoe caddy or on a shoe rack, or in labeled shoeboxes stacked on the closet floor.

• **Turn to deep storage.** Seasonal clothes—such as winter coats and heavy sweaters or summer beachwear—can be neatly packed in plastic bins, sealed in large garment bags, or piled in collapsible canvas storage boxes and kept in your attic or basement, or even under your bed. When you choose a location, make sure that it is free of excess moisture. Use cedar products to deter moths. Removing these items from your closet frees up space for the current season's wardrobe. Special-occasion clothes can be hung in an infrequently used closet.

• **Divide and conquer.** Install shelf dividers to separate stacks of folded sweaters, sweatshirts, or casual pants. The dividers will prevent the piles from toppling over one another or onto the floor. For bulky sweaters, try to limit the stack to only two or three items.

• **Containerize and control.** Storing small items like scarves, caps, mittens, and belts loosely on closet shelves takes up more space than is necessary, and makes it hard to see what you own. Instead, sort and organize them in clear plastic boxes, stacking bins or trays, or a portable drawer unit placed on the closet floor.

• **Go to the wall.** Hooks, as long as you don't overload them, are great for holding belts and handbags or bathrobes, nightgowns, and pajamas. You can install a valet hook or pull-out rod outside your closet door for hanging incoming dry cleaning or your outfit for the next day. Special racks keep ties neat, pressed, and out of the way until you need them. Similar racks can be used for belts.

I don't have enough drawer space.

If your budget and the size of your bedroom permit, the easiest solution is to add a dresser or chest of drawers. Or, if your bedroom is small, you can replace a short dresser with a taller one that offers more drawer space but has the same footprint. The area under your bed is wasted space full of potential. If you want to replace your bed along with reorganizing your bedroom storage, you can purchase a bed with built-in drawers, which add considerable storage for folded clothes. On the following page are some additional strategies for storing items normally kept in drawers. Remember to sort through your drawers and remove clothing you no longer wear.

Organizing Solutions:

• **Go under the bed.** Rather than replace your existing bed with one that has built-in drawers, you can store sweaters, T-shirts, and other folded clothing on rolling carts or in flat, plastic containers made especially for use under a bed. If using carts or other containers that do not come with covers, enclose your clothes in zippered, clear plastic storage bags first.

• **Add shelves.** Shelving units are not as deep as dressers and come in many sizes. Perhaps you can accommodate shelves under a window or in a corner of your bedroom. Some units come with doors, so you can conceal clothing rather than have it on constant display. If you are stacking folded sweaters and pants, use shelf dividers to keep the piles neat.

• **Go portable.** Freestanding drawer units with wheels can be rolled into your closet or another convenient spot near the bedroom. These units come in many shapes, sizes, and colors, and some have stackable bins or storage cubes.

• **Emphasize versatility.** If you like to have seating in your bedroom, add a chest with a flat top or a bench or other piece of furniture that also offers space for storing clothes, accessories, or shoes.

tips

A collapsible garment rack is a great accessory to use when preparing for a vacation or business trip. As you choose them, hang your travel outfits on the rack. You'll see at a glance what you have and what you need, and storing them on the rack will help you keep them clean until you're ready to travel.

Problem:

I have plenty of drawer space, but everything is in disarray.

Even if you have enough space for folded clothing and accessories, it is easy for everything to get disorganized. Keep in mind that the clutter could be concealing not only items that need to be handy but also those that you no longer use and should be discarded. After you've weeded out what you'll never wear, try the solutions on the following page for keeping your clothes neat and orderly.

tips   An attractive dish, box, or basket placed on top of your dresser is a great place for holding your wallet, your keys, your watch, and the bracelet or ring you like to wear every day.

Organizing Solutions:

- **Arrange by category.** Organize drawers according to the way you get dressed. Depending on the size of your drawers, the top one can hold underwear and socks, followed by sweaters and shirts, then pants, in the drawers below. Reserve the bottom drawer for clothes you wear on weekends or only occasionally. Try to limit the contents of a drawer to one or two categories of clothing unless your drawers are particularly generous. Some items, such as socks, you may want to arrange by color or by type, such as everyday socks and athletic socks. Install drawer dividers to keep sock drawers, lingerie drawers, and other sundries drawers in control.

- **Fold and stack smart.** Take into account the dimensions of your drawers and fold your clothes accordingly. Three narrow piles of T-shirts might be better than two wide piles, or two stacks of pants better than three. If your drawers are deep or your stacks of clothing high, use drawer dividers to keep the piles distinct. Always stack like items of clothing—rather than mix shirts and pants, for example—so you can identify the pile from the top item alone.

- **Containerize and protect.** Stockings and pantyhose can be sorted by color and type and kept in lock-top plastic bags. You do not need to discard stockings or pantyhose with small runs or tears—they can be stored in a separate labeled bag and worn under slacks.

- **Containerize and control.** Jewelry can be sorted by category (rings, necklaces, pins, bracelets) and then organized using a number of different accessories. If you have enough space on top of your dresser, a jewelry chest or decorative boxes are a good option. If you are short of space in or on top of your dresser, consider storing your jewelry in a hanging jewelry organizer that can be suspended from a closet pole or mounted on the back of the closet.

tips Keep a separate laundry bag in the closet for dry cleaning. When the bag is full, it's time to go to the cleaners.

Cleaning Your Closet

Time required: 1 day

You'll need to set aside at least a day for this project. Before or after determining what clothes you want to keep and what items you can discard, you'll want to select the organizing accessories (page 134) that will work best for your storage needs.

1   Empty the contents of your closet and put everything on the bed. For each item, ask yourself: Does it fit? Will I really wear it again? Is it in style? Is it in good condition?

2   Put clothing and accessories that you no longer wear in separate garbage bags—one for donations, another for discards. Clothes in need of cleaning go in the laundry basket or into a separate bag for the dry cleaner. Clothes that require mending or alterations should be placed in another bag. If it's difficult to decide whether or not to keep a shirt or a pair of shoes or any other item, try it on. If you don't feel comfortable or like the way you look, chances are that you will never wear the item again.

3   If it's winter and you have swimming suits in your closet—or it's summer and ski clothes are taking up hanging space—store these off-season clothes in plastic containers or garment bags in another closet or in a storage unit under your bed.

You will need all or some of the following:

Garbage bags

Laundry basket

Garment bags or plastic storage containers

Vacuum cleaner and other cleaning supplies

Closet organizers such as replacement closet pole, shoe caddy or shoe shelves, hooks or tie racks, portable drawer units, and shelf dividers

New hangers

Cedar blocks or bags of cedar shavings

4   You should be left with the clothes you know you will wear regularly. Sort them into categories: pants, shirts, slacks, suits, handbags, ties, and shoes. Depending on your wardrobe, you may also want to divide it into work clothes and casual clothes, or work clothes and dress clothes.

5   Vacuum the closet, then clean the walls with soap and warm water.

6   Install the closet organizers you have chosen. Before you put all the items away, come up with an optimal strategy. If you have too many hanging clothes and plenty of shelf space in your closet or drawer space in your dresser, you may want to remove casual pants and knit shirts from hangers, fold them, and put them on the shelves or in the drawers. Or, the opposite may be true—you have a dearth of shelf or drawer space but plenty of room for hangers.

7   Group each category of clothing—all sweaters, all hanging pants, all folded pants, all handbags, all shoes. If one category is particularly large, you may want to break it down by color or into other groupings, such as dress shoes, everyday shoes, and athletic shoes. Replace any bent or broken hangers, or use a more appropriate hanger for a particular garment.

8   When the closet is half filled, stop and take a look. If it feels right, continue. If not, rethink and adjust the organization. When you're finished, hang a cedar block or bag of cedar shavings. Cedar deters moths and gives the closet a pleasant aroma.

Maintenance Strategies

Always put clothing away in the category and location where it belongs.

Go through your closet periodically—a good time is when the season changes—and dispose of clothes you no longer wear while also replacing one season's wardrobe with the next.

When hanging clothes you've just worn, empty the pockets. Fasten the top button of shirts and blouses, especially those made of silk, so they'll stay on the hangers.

Choosing the right hanger

You may be hanging all of your clothes on flimsy wire hangers from the dry cleaner. The fact is, wire hangers, while ubiquitous and, let's face it, free, are not suitable for long-term use. Good hangers can keep your clothing looking better, longer. Here are the hangers available, and some tips for using them.

- Notched hangers. For strappy dresses and tops, look for notched hangers that will keep them in place. If you don't have notched hangers, a couple of clothespins on the outside corners will prevent straps from sliding off.

- Padded hangers. These soft, fabric hangers won't snag or rip delicates, and help keep silky items from slipping off the hanger. Perfect for lingerie and silk blouses.

- Skirt hangers. Typically made from metal, the sliding clips on these hangers can accommodate skirts with different width waistlines and are usually lined with rubber or fabric for a good grip.

- Trouser hangers. This clamp hanger grasps a pair of pants by the cuffs, discouraging wrinkles.

- Wooden hangers. Good-quality wood hangers are a great investment for keeping your clothing looking great longer. A wooden shirt hanger has contoured shoulders to keep shirts looking nice between wearings, as does a suit hanger, which also comes with a bar across the bottom rung for holding pants in place.

Your nightstand

What you like to keep at your bedside will determine which type of nightstand is best for you or how you want to reorganize an existing nightstand. Here are some ideas and solutions for outfitting the perfect nightstand.

- For copious amounts of books and magazines, you need a nightstand with shelves. If you keep pills and medications at your bedside, your nightstand should have a drawer.

- Perhaps you like to work on a hobby or craft project in bed. If your nightstand cannot accommodate all of your supplies, put them in pull-out drawers or plastic storage containers that will fit under the bed.

- The top of your nightstand should be reserved for a reading light (unless your light is wall-mounted) and any other essential items such as a flashlight, tissues, pen and pad, alarm clock, or glass of water. Earrings, watch, and glasses or a contact lens holder can be placed in an attractive small dish, box, or basket for safekeeping.

- As much as possible, keep the items on top of your nightstand to a minimum. You don't want clutter to be what you see when you go to bed and again when you wake in the morning.

Cleaning Your Drawers

Time required: 1 day

You'll need to set aside at least a day for this project. Before or after determining what clothes you want to keep and what items you can discard, you'll want to select the organizing accessories (page 134) that will work best for your storage needs.

1   Empty the contents of your drawers and put everything on the bed. For each item, ask yourself: Does it fit? Will I really wear it again? Is it in style? Is it in good condition?

2   Put clothing and accessories that you no longer wear in separate garbage bags—one for donations, another for discards. Clothes in need of cleaning go in the laundry basket or into a separate bag for the dry cleaner. Clothes that require mending or alterations should be placed in another bag. If you're having a hard time deciding whether or not to keep a shirt, a scarf, or a piece of costume jewelry, try it on. If you don't like the way you look or the item no longer fits properly, you'll probably never wear it again.

3   If it's winter and you have shorts and swimming suits in your drawers—or it's summer and heavy wool sweaters are taking up drawer space—store these off-season clothes in plastic containers or garment bags in another closet or in a storage unit under your bed.

You will need all or some of the following:

Garbage bags

Laundry basket

Garment bags or plastic storage containers

Vacuum cleaner and other cleaning supplies

Drawer liners

Drawer dividers

4   You should be left with the clothes you will wear regularly. Sort them into categories: underwear, stockings, socks, lingerie, short-sleeve and long-sleeve T-shirts, pajamas. You may also want to divide the categories further, say, into work clothes and casual clothes, or work clothes and athletic clothes.

5   Vacuum all the drawers and clean them with soap and warm water. After the drawers have dried completely, cut liners to fit. If you like, install drawer dividers to keep the piles of clothes in place.

6   Before you fill the drawers, come up with the best system for your wardrobe. If you have too many folded clothes and plenty of closet space, you may want to hang casual pants and long-sleeved T-shirts in the closet. Or maybe you've gained drawer space to accommodate items from your closet shelf that belong with the categories in your drawers.

7   If possible, place only one or two categories in a drawer, and organize drawers according to the way you get dressed. The top one could hold underwear and socks, followed by sweaters and shirts, then pants, in the drawers below. Reserve the lowest drawer for those items you wear only occasionally.

8   When you've filled half of the drawers, look at the arrangement. If it feels right, continue. If not, rethink the organization and make adjustments. Do not overstuff drawers and be sure that you can open and close each drawer with ease.

Maintenance Strategies

When removing a sweater or shirt from a drawer, try not to disrupt the whole pile of clothes. When returning it, fold it neatly and put it back in the same place.

Always return laundered or dry-cleaned items to their correct place in the drawers.

Go through your drawers periodically—say, when the season changes—and dispose of clothes and accessories you no longer wear.

In addition to the storage containers and other accessories listed here—available at housewares stores and home-improvement outlets, as well as by mail order—you can add furniture that will augment your bedroom storage. An armoire is useful if your closet storage is limited. A bed with built-in drawers can hold folded clothes, linens, and other items unable to fit on closet shelves or in your chest of drawers. A low chest with a flat top or a bench or other piece of furniture with storage capacity can do double duty—for both seating and holding clothes or shoes. Shelving units come in many sizes to fit under windows and into corners.

Many stores and catalogs carry storage systems that can be customized for your closet. They include closet poles, modular shelves, drawer units, and other handy containers. Some systems require that you install them yourself; others can be installed for you.

Drawer dividers and organizers. Dividers are essentially slip-in barriers that help keep piles of socks, stockings, and underwear from creeping out of place. Organizers come in all shapes and sizes and are simply slipped inside the drawer, creating a protective and organized environment for small accessories such as jewelry.

Freestanding drawers. Often mounted on wheels, such portable drawers can be stored in the closet under hanging clothes or in a storage area near the bedroom.

Garment bags. Off-season clothes and special-occasion clothes can also be kept protected in hanging garment bags placed at one end of your closet or in another storage closet in your home.

Hanging closet pole. This pole hangs from your existing pole and accommodates short clothes such as shirts and folded pants.

Hanging plastic jewelry organizers. Suspended from a closet pole or hung on a wall, these organizers have many small pockets to hold necklaces, earrings, and bracelets.

Hanging shelves. Usually made from fabric or vinyl, these flexible shelves come in varying widths and heights, and hang from the closet rod to provide extra storage space for sweaters or shoes.

Hat racks. You can hang a rack for hats and caps from the ceiling or closet pole or on the wall or over a door.

Hooks. There are myriad options here, from rows of hooks that you can mount on your wall or door for hanging belts and bags, to single large valet hooks sturdy enough to hold heavier items.

Shelf dividers. Usually made of heavy-duty acrylic, dividers slide onto shelves and hold stacks of folded shirts or sweaters in place.

Shoe caddies and shelves. Caddies, available in different fabrics and sizes, can be hung on the inside of a door or from a closet pole or can be mounted on a wall. Shoe shelves, which stand on the floor, are angled to give your shoes optimum visibility in your closet. Other types of shelves and holders are made to be hung from the back of a closet or on a wall.

Stackable storage bins and stackable drawers. If you are short of drawer space or closet shelves, bins and drawers are ideal for holding clothing and accessories. Slide them in the closet under your hanging clothes or use sizes that will fit neatly on closet shelves.

Tie and belt racks. There are many different types, including wooden or plastic, and wall mounted or racks on hangers.

Under-the-bed storage containers. Clear plastic containers with tight-fitting lids, rolling carts and drawers, and flat baskets keep clothes, linens, and other items organized and out-of-sight under the bed.

Zippered, clear plastic storage bags. These lightweight bags in various sizes can be used for storing off-season clothing or spare blankets on closet shelves. They are ideal for protecting clothes that you are storing in an open under-the-bed cart or basket.

the **BATHROOM**

Rare is the house or apartment that has a large bathroom. Therefore, because bathrooms are fairly small, efficient use of space is crucial.

Most people face two basic organizational problems in the bathroom: lack of sufficient storage and ineffective use of storage. Fortunately, bathroom storage can be increased and made more efficient by applying some key strategies and using some practical accessories.

To decide which areas of your bathroom need attention, answer the questionnaire on page 140. If you are eager to start reorganizing, try the simple project on page 148 that is guaranteed to help you get started in clearing your bathroom clutter.

Bathroom

questionnaire   * * *

1   **Do you sometimes have to store bathroom necessities like medicines or paper products in a closet outside your bathroom?**

2   **Is the bathroom windowsill or area around the tub or sink littered with toiletries?**

3   **Do damp towels fail to dry because you lack sufficient space to hang them?**

If you answered yes to any of these questions, you lack enough storage space in your bathroom. No matter how small your bathroom, you can find ways to increase the storage dramatically. For tips and solutions, turn to page 143.

4   **Is it difficult for you and other members of your family to find their favorite shampoo or a new toothbrush in bathroom cabinets?**

5   **Do you make a special trip to purchase hair conditioner, lipstick, or sunblock but later discover that you own the same product?**

6   **Do you feel you spend more time than necessary in the bathroom to accomplish your morning routine?**

7   **Do you need to clean up bathroom clutter before you entertain guests?**

A yes response to any of these questions indicates that your bathroom is likely in disarray. Go to page 145 for solutions.

Common Bathroom Problems

Now that you have a better idea of the parts of your bathroom that need reorganizing, it's time to focus on specific solutions. You'll also want to review the many accessories (page 152) you can use to maximize bathroom storage.

My bathroom doesn't have enough storage space.

Any solution to a lack of storage space must begin with taking a look at what you have in your bathroom cabinets or arrayed on various surfaces. If months have gone by since you last cleaned out your bathroom storage, you may find expired prescriptions, empty bottles of shampoo or lotion, or products that you do not intend to use. Once you've discarded all these items, you're ready to consider how to increase the storage to accommodate what you want to keep.

Turn to deep storage. Many people like to purchase products such as cotton swabs, toilet paper, lotion, and shampoo in large containers or in bulk. Although this is a prudent financial strategy, it can present a storage challenge. If your bathroom storage is limited, keep only the supplies you need immediately in the bathroom, and store the overflow in a closet outside the bathroom or on the topmost shelf of your linen closet. Rather than try to find places in the bathroom to store large bottles of lotion, shampoo, or conditioner, transfer portions to small bottles or containers that will fit in the shower-area medicine cabinet.

Call for backup. If the inside of your bathroom door is empty—and you lack places to hang damp towels—you can install at least two towel bars or a hanging rack of towel bars. The door is also the ideal spot for hooks, useful for hanging bathrobes as well as towels. Or you might consider hanging a clear plastic shoe organizer and filling the pockets with bath and beauty supplies.

Add cabinets. Like the kitchen, the bathroom lends itself to the use of many different types of cabinets, since you don't need to reserve the spare wall and floor space for other purposes. Although pedestal sinks are attractive, you might consider replacing your pedestal sink with a sink and sur- rounding vanity. The wall above the toilet is another spot where a cabinet can be mounted. If you have a free corner, you can tuck a corner cabinet or corner shelf unit into this wedge of space.

Maximize cabinet interiors. Take a look at the backs of your cabinet doors and see if you have enough room to add cups, hooks, or racks to hold toothpaste, razors, or cosmetics. The cabinets need to be deep enough so that the doors close after the accessory is mounted. A spice rack of the right size might do the job as well. Horizontal holders for toothpaste can be attached under a shelf of the medicine cabinet.

Control the small stuff. A seemingly infinite array of hooks, hangers, and shelves can be installed in the bathroom to hold small items. Dispensers for soap and shampoo can be mounted in the shower or on the wall next to the sink. Holders on suction cups that adhere to tile help keep soap dry; hooks on suction cups hold wash- cloths. Shower caddies hanging from the shower- head or mounted in a corner of the shower hold soap, shampoo, and washcloths. Toothbrushes and toothpaste are at the ready, when slipped in a wall holder or stowed in a sink caddy. A sturdy hook for a blow dryer can be installed near an outlet. You can find lidded baskets that will fit on top of the toilet tank—a practical location for storing extra rolls of toilet tissue.

Go portable. Portable plastic storage units come in narrow widths and can be squeezed in small places, offering two or more additional drawers for everything from toiletries to extra towels. You can stow all of your cosmetics in a portable caddy with a handle and store the caddy in a closet outside the bathroom.

Problem:

_____

I have enough storage space in my bathroom, but everything is in disarray.

If the insides of your cabinets are cluttered and every available surface is occupied by a hodge-podge of toiletries, you probably need to weed out empty containers of shampoo, conditioner, and lotion, as well as dispose of any products members of your household will never use. The next step is to prioritize the remaining items and find the best places to store them so everyone can locate them easily.

Organizing Solutions:

• **Arrange by category.** No matter what kind of storage you use—whether wall cabinets or under-the-sink stacking drawers—keep like items together. Group all makeup and cosmetics, all spare toothbrushes and toothpaste tubes, all lotions, all first-aid supplies, all vitamins. Use lazy Susans or expanding shelves in cabinets or some of the containers suggested here so each category stays neat and visible.

• **Make essentials accessible.** It's time for a brief experiment: Go in your bathroom, stand at the sink, and grab hold of your toothbrush, toothpaste, and dental floss, or your facial soap and washcloth, or your razor and shaving cream. If these and other essentials are not at arm's reach, you need to rearrange them. The best place for items your family uses daily is the medicine cabinet above your sink. Situated at eye level, it is the most accessible cabinet in the bathroom. The shelves are usually adjustable, so you'll want to raise or lower them to accommodate razors, shaving cream, dental floss, prescriptions, and any other frequently used products. If the cabinet is not large enough for toothbrushes, mount a wall holder for them or use a sink caddy.

• **Containerize and control.** Use clear plastic containers and lock-top plastic bags to house small items like hair ties and bobby pins. Or you can store such small necessities as nail files and scissors in the compartments of drawer dividers. Transparent jars and canisters are practical receptacles for cotton balls and swabs. If your household does not have a well-stocked first-aid kit, this might be the time to assemble one, so everyone in the household knows what it includes and where to find it in an emergency. If your children's bath toys wind up scattered at the bottom of the bathtub or around the floor, corral them in a mesh bag that can be hung from a hook suctioned to the tile wall.

• **Gang appliances.** Special wall mounts are available for holding hair dryers, electric razors, and curling irons. Install them near an electrical outlet. Keeping appliances within sight is preferable to shoving them in a cabinet or drawer, where they wind up in a nest of tangled electrical cords.

• **Maximize shower space.** Shower caddies come in a range of sizes. Some hang from the showerhead; others can be mounted in a corner. Mesh caddies with compartments hang from the shower curtain rod. If all family members use the same bathroom, purchase a large caddy so everyone can have their own compartment or shelf for storing their preferred shampoo, soap, or other bath accessories.

The linen closet

In most homes, the linen closet is either in the bathroom or in an area adjacent to the bathroom. Here are some practical tips for keeping a tidy and well-organized linen closet.

- Stack towels by size and type.

- Place infrequently used towels, such as beach towels, and guest, on a less accessible shelf.

- Stack sheets and pillowcases for each bedroom together, separating them by either a shelf or by separate piles. Or, stack by type—all the sheets for single beds in one stack, all the sheets for queen beds in another. This will save time when changing sheets.

- Keep extra blankets and quilts folded neatly and protected in zippered bags.

- Accessorize using closet and cabinet organizers such as lazy Susans, shelf expanders, and hanging door organizers to accommodate medicines, toiletries, and other small items that cannot be accommodated in bathroom storage.

Organizing Your Medicine Cabinet

Time required: 1–2 hours

Your medicine cabinet is the most important cabinet in your bathroom. Situated over the sink, it is the best place to store essential items, from toothpaste to important prescriptions, that you and your family need at your fingertips every day. Before you begin the project, review the list of organizing accessories on page 152 and choose those that suit your cabinet and its contents. You'll also want to consider if you need to remove toothbrushes and bars of soap from the cabinet to gain additional space. If so, you can purchase wall-mounted holders or sink caddies for these items.

1 Remove everything from your medicine cabinet. Discard expired prescriptions and products you and other household members never use. Put duplicate and surplus items like extra boxes of cotton swabs and bandages in a pile for alternate storage.

2 Divide the remaining items into categories: medications, oral hygiene, first aid, shaving equipment. If the space in your cabinet is limited, restrict the contents to toiletries that need to be kept near the sink. Put cotton swabs and balls and other small objects into small jars or canisters.

3 Clean the interior of the cabinet, as well as the door, with soap and water.

You will need:

Garbage bag

Cleaning supplies

Accessories such as hanging shelves or drawers or back-of-the-cabinet organizers

4   Install any accessories you've chosen under the
     shelves or on the back of the door. If necessary,
     adjust the height of the shelves to accommodate
     containers of varying sizes.

5   Keeping like items together, designate areas for
     each category: oral hygiene (toothbrushes, tooth-
     paste, dental floss); shaving equipment (razors,
     shaving cream); over-the-counter medications
     (aspirin, antibiotic cream, bandages).

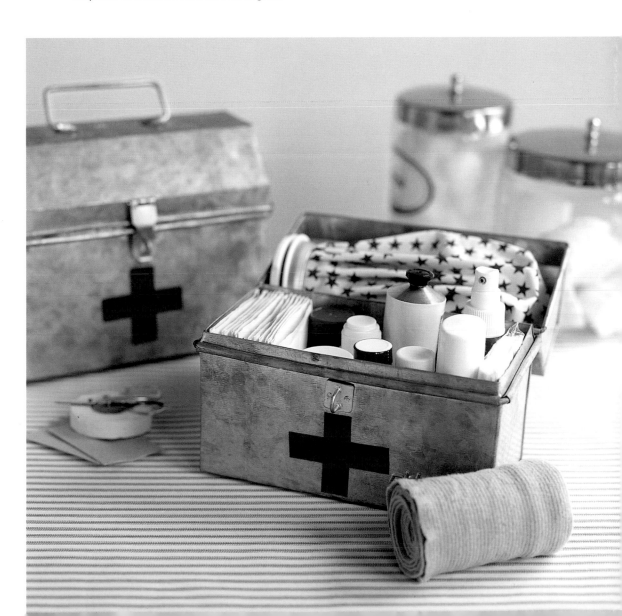

Bathrooms used by young children can be outfitted for safety and convenience. Here are a few solutions for addressing kids' organizational needs in the bathroom.

- Install low towel racks so children can hang their own towels and robes.

- Create a place for bath toys. Either designate a shelf in the cabinet, or look for a waterproof mesh bag that suctions to the shower wall or hangs from the water faucet.

- Install a special, low-mounted holder for toothbrush, toothpaste, and plastic cup.

- Store safely. Keep all medicines and toxic items out of reach on high shelves or in locked cabinets.

The following accessories, mentioned throughout the chapter, are relatively inexpensive and can be found in hardware and housewares stores or can be mail-ordered from catalogs.

Appliance holders. Some holders are made especially for blow dryers. Others can accommodate multiple appliances, such as blow dryers and electric shavers.

Clear jars and canisters. Available in plastic or glass, these containers can be filled with cotton balls, swabs, and other small items. You can find containers that will fit on the narrow shelves of medicine cabinets.

Clear plastic shoe organizers. Hang an organizer on the back of the door and use the compartments to hold bath and beauty supplies.

Corner cabinets and shelves. Chances are that at least one corner of your bathroom can accommodate corner storage, either on the floor or high on the wall.

Cosmetic organizers. A wide variety of trays, some of them stacking, are made for holding makeup. Also available are specialized organizers for items such as lipstick. If bathroom storage is tight, a caddy with all your cosmetics can be kept in the linen closet or another closet near the bathroom and brought out as needed.

Drawer and cabinet organizers. Drawer dividers and expanding shelves and lazy Susans for cabinet shelves are ideal for holding categories of toiletries. Small holders for toothpaste tubes and small drawer units can be mounted under cabinet shelves. Various cups, hooks, and racks can be attached to the back of cabinets for storing toothpaste, razors, and cosmetics.

Hooks. There is a hook for every purpose: suction-cup hooks for hanging washcloths in the shower, sturdy hooks for bathrobes and towels, hooks made especially for hanging appliances. Exercise moderation when installing hooks—you don't want your bathroom to look like a retail display.

Plastic bottles and pump dispensers. These are particularly useful if you purchase shampoo, lotion, and other liquids in bulk. Transfer small amounts to these convenient containers, and stow the main supply outside the bathroom.

Shower caddies. Rigid wire or plastic caddies hang from the shower head. Some units, in the form of baskets or shelves, can be mounted in the corner of the shower/bathtub area. Larger mesh caddies hang from the shower rod. All can be used to keep soap, shampoo, cream rinse, sponges, and other bathing items organized and accessible.

Stackable bins and pull-out stackable drawers. Available in a variety of heights and widths, these containers can fit in a floor cabinet or vanity or be placed directly on the floor. A floor unit is a good location for cleaning supplies.

Suction-cup hangers and organizers. Hooks, soap dispensers, mesh bags for kids' bath toys, and holders of other types come with suction cups that can be affixed to tile walls. These versatile organizers do not require permanent installation and can be removed or relocated as desired.

Toothbrush holders. If your medicine cabinet is too full to accommodate toothbrushes, install a wall-mounted holder near the cabinet and sink, or purchase a sink caddy. Some holders have a place for a tube of toothpaste and a cup or two.

Towel bars. Individual bars or racks of bars can be installed on the back of the bathroom door or on bathroom walls if space is available. Some racks hang from the top of the door, so you don't need to mar the surface with hardware.

STORAGE *and* UTILITY ROOMS

Extra space in your home—whether in a basement, attic, garage, or utility room—can be your organizational salvation. Or, it can give you some of your biggest storage headaches.

The key to making these rooms work for you is organizing and safeguarding your belongings, while also improving the functionality of areas devoted to specific activities such as laundry. Since such storage fills up fast, you need to be proactive in keeping it tidy. This can be challenging because the rooms are out of sight—hence the adage "out of sight, out of mind." In many homes, they tend to be a dumping ground for all the stuff people don't want to see but can't bring themselves to throw away. Perhaps this phenomenon sounds all too familiar to you.

Each extra storage area comes with inherent concerns. If you park one or more cars in your garage, floor space is at a premium. This means that efficient strategies for using wall and ceiling space are crucial. Basements, since they are usually one large room, often benefit from centrally placed storage units such as cabinets or shelving, which enable you to maximize efficient use of the floor space and create access corridors. You may also rely on your basement for multiple activities: as work space and laundry room, for example.

Before you launch into an organizational makeover of your basement storage, you may want to rearrange other parts of the space so it is more efficient for all purposes. Similarly, if you have a utility room that contains laundry facilities, controlling the clutter of clothes and cleaning supplies will allow you to create additional storage opportunities.

How you use your attic depends on its accessibility. Some attics have fold-down stairs that are narrow and difficult to navigate, or have low ceilings. If either is true of your attic, you will not want to store large or frequently needed items there. Walk-in attics are easier to access and often more spacious. Just be sure that the attic floor can support your weight and that of the objects you intend to store.

One important element distinguishes these areas from other parts of your home: the influence of climate. Basements, garages, laundry rooms, and unfinished utility rooms can be damp; attics can be very hot in summer and cold in winter. You will want to consider any special conditions and make minor improvements before storing your possessions (see page 167). Because all these areas can be dusty and dirty, anything valuable—past years' taxes, off-season clothes, antique furniture, family keepsakes—needs to be contained properly or otherwise protected.

Despite the differences between these spaces, many of the same organizing concepts apply—so you'll want to answer the questionnaire on page 160 before deciding where to turn your attention. If you are eager to get started, review the projects beginning on page 168. One is sure to have an impact on improving your storage and utility rooms.

Storage and Utility Rooms
questionnaire ✳ ✳ ✳

1 : **Do piles of boxes make it hard for you and your family members to maneuver in your storage area or utility room?**

2 : **Did you once intend to use this space for multiple purposes, but now find it too hard to reach your sports equipment or do projects at your workbench?**

3 : **Would you like to carve out a small work area, but the space seems filled?**

If you answered yes to any of these questions, you probably don't have enough storage space. On page 163 you'll find ways to maximize the space.

4 : **Is it hard to find anything stored in your storage area?**

5 : **Do you avoid using your extra storage because it contains a jumble of containers and loose objects?**

6 : **Are you unsure about what you have stored in the recesses of your attic, basement, or garage?**

If you answered yes to any of these questions, your storage area is in disarray. Turn to page 165 for solutions.

common Storage and Utility Room Problems

Whether you lack sufficient space, or just need to streamline a cluttered storage area, here are some solutions that will help you clear the clutter. Turn to page 174 for some hard-working accessories.

I don't have enough storage space.

There is no better way to gain storage space than to sort through your belongings and weed out what you and your family no longer need. If you are holding on to spare household furniture, ask yourself if it is really worth saving for a potential future use or if it is needlessly taking up valuable space. If you do want to keep it—and the furniture has cabinets or drawers—use them for storage.

Once your assessment is complete, you may want to consider adding a storage area for a specific function. For example, a tool shed can be a good investment if you are an avid gardener. Ready-made sheds are available in a range of shapes, sizes, and styles. You can probably find one that will fit into a corner of your yard or another unobtrusive spot. Before you decide to add storage, however, apply some of the solutions below to your existing storage.

tips Always store with safety in mind. Heavy items should be kept close to the ground. You don't want to reach for them on tall shelves and risk being hurt by a falling box or a hefty tool. Set up a separate shelf unit to store household chemicals such as paint, paint thinners, oils and lubricants, fertilizers, and other flammable and poisonous materials. Read the labels and follow any special storage instructions.

Arrange by category. Divide the space into sections, one for each storage category. All carpentry tools belong near the garage or basement workbench, for instance, and all sports equipment in their own area, on shelves, hung from the wall, or placed in suitable bins. Boxes of holiday and other special-occasion decorations should be ganged in the attic and separated from containers or garment bags holding off-season clothes. Organizing in categories will help you gain space not only for storage but also for a work area dedicated to a particular activity such as laundry or craft projects.

Go to the wall. Since you do not need to preserve empty wall space in these rooms for décor, you can fill the walls with shelves, cabinets, and pegboard. A garage, basement, or utility room is also the place to put old furniture to good use. Kitchen cabinets or office shelves that you would otherwise discard can be hung on the wall of the laundry area and used for cleaning supplies. Pegboard with hooks is great for holding carpentry or gardening tools, allowing you to see what you own.

Add floor storage. Large, open areas such as basements and walk-in attics need to be given some structure so you can avoid cluttering the space. Old chests of drawers or bookshelves may be just what you need to create a central storage island. Purchased shelving is inexpensive and can be arranged in the center of the space.

Go high. If your ceilings are sufficiently tall enough, hang hooks in your garage to hold bicycles or lawn maintenance gear, or a closet pole or old broomstick attached to the ceiling joists in the basement or attic to hold off-season clothing. If ceiling space is particularly generous, consider building a simple loft, which could easily expand the storage space by 50 percent.

Fill wasted space. In addition to regarding stored furniture like chests of drawers as opportunities for extra storage, you can use suitcases to hold off-season clothes or fragile items such as well-packed glassware or heirlooms, especially if you travel infrequently. Smaller suitcases can be nested inside larger ones.

I have enough storage space, but everything is in disarray.

The word *disarray* suggests that you likely do not know what you are storing. If this is the case, you need to go through everything and jettison items you no longer need or use. Be alert for such belongings as broken furniture or gardening tools, mildewed books, or paint cans containing minuscule amounts of paint. Once you've disposed of them, sort what's left into categories and try some of the suggestions on the following page for controlling the clutter.

Clean and improve. Reorganizing offers an opportunity to clean and paint the entire area. This may be desirable if you also use a portion of your basement, garage, or utility room as a work space. You're more likely to take an active, ongoing role in keeping the area organized if you get a clean start. You may also need to improve the lighting, not only to illuminate all corners of the space but also to provide task lighting over a workbench or in a laundry area.

Make essentials accessible. Store the most infrequently used items on high shelves or in the back. These include boxes of off-season clothes that you've removed from bedroom closets or special-occasion serving ware that you cannot accommodate in your dining room. Belongings you and your family need to access regularly—such as bicycles and other sports equipment—should be toward the front and at eye level. Make sure that you allow walkways so you can reach everything, including the containers in areas you regard as deep storage.

Arrange efficiently. The way you organize items should depend on what you're storing and how you're using the space. A small workbench with cabinets set against a wall in the garage or basement can do double duty as work space and storage. You'll want to place it near the power supply if you use power tools or need to recharge batteries or battery-operated tools. Wall-mounted magnetic strips or pegboard with hooks, above the bench, can hold tools. If you do a lot of work on cars, use a portable tool cart to keep everything at your fingertips. Similarly, if gardening is your passion, a bucket with a handle makes an excellent repository for small tools such as clippers, trowels, and gardening gloves. When you want to garden, you're ready to go. For storing and toting a larger number of tools, you can use a wheeled cart with holders for rakes, shovels, and long-handled implements, as well as pouches for small items.

If your garage or basement is unfinished and therefore has exposed studs, you can set long-handled tools between the studs and hold them safely in place with ropes, bungee cords, or wooden slats. A loft added to a tall-ceilinged garage is also a good place for these implements, as well as for a range of possessions, from camping gear to items relegated to deep storage.

Continued →

• **Containerize and protect.** Papers such as tax records and family memorabilia should be stored in airtight, waterproof containers. Fragile belongings—holiday decorations, heirlooms, dishware—must be packed carefully in sturdy boxes. Square containers are the best choice because they stack well. Choose transparent ones so you can see the contents. Fabric also merits special handling. Use a garment rack on wheels or mount a closet pole from the ceiling joists for hanging clothes. Rather than plastic garment bags, use cloth bags, which allow the garments to breathe.

• **Avoid overstuffing.** You may be tempted to cram objects into your attic or boxes into your utility room. Instead, exercise restraint and maintain walkways so you can reach everything, and try not to overfill shelves and other storage furniture so you can always find what you're looking for and do not create a safety hazard.

• **Label and record.** Whether your stored items are in boxes or bags, you need to label each container with a description of the contents. Paints or similar substances with a limited shelf life should be labeled by date as well.

Climate Control

Considering climate control and other environmental conditions should be the first task on your list when reorganizing your basement, garage, attic, or utility room storage. Before placing items in any of these spaces, be sure they will not be damaged by fluctuations in temperature and can be protected from moisture as well as rodents and insects. Here are some additional tips for protecting your belongings.

- If dampness is common in your area and your basement, garage, or utility room is unfinished, you can install an elevated floor. Alternatively, you can use wooden pallets to lift important possessions such as antique furniture or boxes of books.

- A dehumidifier is useful for removing moisture in the air. If you have a drain or sump pump in your basement, purchase a dehumidifier that drains automatically rather than one with a reservoir that needs to be emptied manually.

- Attics can be oppressively hot in summer. To promote air circulation and help reduce the temperature, you can add a fan.

- Avoid storing anything within three feet of a clothes washer, hot water heater, furnace, or boiler. Not only do you want to prevent your belongings from being damaged by leaks, but you want have access to these major appliances.

- Periodically check floors, walls, and ceilings in basements, garages, and utility rooms for leaks, either from the outside or from household plumbing, and make prompt repairs.

- Store clothes in cloth garment bags rather than plastic bags. Plastic encourages moisture to collect on clothes. Conversely, use airtight waterproof containers for important papers.

- Fill any holes in the walls or ceilings with steel wool to deter mice. Tuck cedar blocks or bags of cedar shavings in garment bags to discourage moths.

Organizing Your Sports Equipment

Time required: 2–3 hours

Skateboards, tennis rackets, skis, boots, and poles, soccer balls, bicycles—sports equipment can easily get out of hand, especially if you have an active family with diverse interests. There are many organizing accessories such as shelving and large containers that you can use to keep everything under control. Bicycles, for instance, can be suspended from the ceiling from large hooks or hung on wall-mounted brackets that can also accommodate helmets. Before you start the project, review the list of accessories on page 174 and choose those that will work best for you.

1   Collect all the sports equipment lying around the house. Don't overlook anything in your car.

2   Sort the equipment by sport, taking the time to examine the condition. Items that are broken beyond repair, worn out, do not fit, or are no longer used should be put in separate piles for repair or donation, or in the trash. Further sort the equipment by season—skis and poles and snowboards in one pile, baseballs and baseball bats in another. Establish a pile for year-round equipment.

3   Install the accessories you need to hold the current season's or year-round equipment. Designate another area and appropriate accessories for off-season equipment. If family members participate in team sports, items can be kept in a gym bag, ready to go.

You will need all or some of the following:

Garbage bag

Shelves, storage bins, hooks, racks, and other organizing accessories

Gym bags

Blank labels or masking tape and permanent marker, or label maker

4   As you load the shelves, bins, hooks, and racks, keep like items together—all hockey equipment in one place, all golf gear in another. Make sure you are satisfied with the arrangement. Create a label for each shelf, bin, hook, or rack.

Maintenance Strategies

Following the labels, always put equipment back in the same location after use. All family members should familiarize themselves with how everything is stored.

Clean and repair equipment at the end of every season before storing it until the next season.

Organizing Your Tools

Time required: 2–3 hours

Even if woodworking is not your hobby, you probably have hammers, screwdrivers, pliers, and drills, along with attendant hardware, that you rely on for simple household repairs. One of the best ways to store tools is on hooks and holders mounted on pegboard, where you can easily see them. The pegboard can be installed above a workbench with drawers, or above shelves or cabinets that you can use for additional storage. If you like, you can paint the pegboard. The same system will work equally well for gardening tools or tools for a special hobby or activity.

Decide where you want to install the pegboard and take the necessary measurements before you go shopping. You'll also want to determine which items you will be hanging and which items you will store in containers, then select the appropriate accessories (page 174). The latter are usually best for hardware such as nails, screws, bolts, and washers.

1   Gather all the tools you want to store. Check kitchen drawers or other locations where commonly used tools like pliers and screwdrivers might be hidden away.

2   Sort the tools and hardware by category. If you have a large tool collection, separate it into hand tools and power tools, then by type. Broken tools that are beyond repair and rusted hardware should be discarded. This is a good time to do any maintenance. Cleaning and lubricating tools will help them work better and extend their life. Arrange all hardware by type and size.

You will need all or some of the following:

Cleaning supplies and lubricant

Pegboard and accompanying hooks, racks, and holders

Plastic or glass jars and/or small-parts organizers

Clear plastic storage containers or stackable drawers

Tool boxes, organizers, or caddies

Lock-top plastic bags

Blank label or masking tape and permanent marker, or label maker

3   Install the pegboard on the wall. Looking at your categories of tools, mount hooks, racks, and other holders on the pegboard in the preferred locations. You want to keep each category—screwdrivers, wrenches, pliers, handsaws—in its own area and arrange the items by size, from large to small or vice versa. Safety equipment such as goggles, masks, and gloves can occupy their own area. Also hang power tools if they are small. Large, heavy tools are best stored on shelves or in drawers, where there is no danger of them falling. All drill bits, screwdriver attachments, and other parts should be kept in a container alongside the appropriate tool. For those tools that you use regularly, you may want to store them in a portable tool box, organizer, or caddy. This way you have a repair kit that is ready to go.

4   Place each type and size of hardware in its own jar or in a drawer or compartment of a small-parts organizer. Depending on the quantity of your hardware, the jars or organizer can go on the workbench or on a nearby shelf or in a cabinet. It is best to leave the top of your workbench or other work surface free of clutter. Put items such as drop cloths and sandpaper on shelves or in cabinets, or in transparent bins or stackable drawers. Roll up extension cords, secure them, and hang them on wall hooks or on the pegboard.

5   You want to keep tool manuals together in an accessible place. They can be slipped into plastic bags and stored in their own container or drawer.

6   Examine your arrangement of tools on the pegboard, as well as the location of other items, and make any adjustments. Using a permanent marker, trace around each tool on the pegboard. Then create a label for each drawer, shelf, or storage bin.

Maintenance Strategies

• Always return a tool to its outlined place on the pegboard or its proper drawer, shelf, or storage bin. Likewise, each container of hardware should be returned to its designated spot.

• When you or a family member use any supplies such as nails or sandpaper, write down the items and replace them on your next trip to the hardware store.

Organizing Your Laundry Room

Time required: 2–3 hours

Perhaps you are fortunate enough to have a dedicated laundry room. Or maybe you have a laundry area in your garage or basement or in another utility room. Regardless of the location, you can probably gain storage space by reorganizing its contents. You can use the extra space for deep storage—as a place to keep infrequently used items from other rooms in the house, including off-season clothes—or you can add accessories that you'll find helpful for doing the laundry, such as drying racks for hand wash or perhaps a narrow cabinet that contains a fold-out ironing board.

Before you go shopping for storage furniture and accessories, decide how you want to improve your laundry room and what you want to store there, and then review the items on page 174. You can find special shelves that fit over a washer's control panel, so cleaning supplies are always handy. Some garment racks and drying racks are foldable and can be stashed out of the way when not in use.

1   Assemble all of your laundry detergents and other supplies. If you're holding on to soaps, fabric softeners, or the like that you'll never use, dispose of them. If you have multiple containers of one product, consolidate your supply into one container.

2   Designate a basket for dirty laundry so family members know exactly where to deposit items that need cleaning. You may also want to hang a couple of laundry bags from hooks—one for clothing to be mended, another for clothing to be taken to the dry cleaner. Or you may prefer to use other categories, such as a basket or bag for especially dirty sports or gardening cloths, another for everyday wear, and yet another for linens.

You will need all or some of the following:

Laundry basket and bags

Hooks

Floor or wall shelves or cabinets

Freestanding or wall-mounted garment racks

Hangers

Iron/ironing board hanger

Cloth garment bags

Zippered, plastic storage bags

3   Decide where you want to install the storage furniture and accessories. You can maximize your wall
space by mounting shelves and cabinets above the
washer/dryer, near the ceiling. Remember to store
infrequently used items on the high shelves. Install
the iron/ironing board hanger, placing it close to
where you will use it. Be sure to leave room for
your garment rack, either on the wall or on the
floor. If you're using the rack for just-cleaned
clothes, you want it near the washer/dryer or ironing board. A rack intended for off-season clothes
should go in an out-of-the-way place.

4   Hang your off-season clothes in garment bags and
place them on the racks. Folded clothes and linens
can go in zippered plastic bags on shelves. Make a
list of the items you've placed in long-term storage
and date the list.

Maintenance Strategies

Use your kitchen shopping list to
note cleaning supplies you need
before they run out.

As soon as clothes emerge from
the dryer or are ironed, distribute
them where they belong, rather than
leaving them piled or hanging in the
laundry room.

The following racks, containers, and other accessories can easily be found in home-improvement stores and specialty catalogs.

Battery organizer. This wall rack holds all sizes of batteries. Some are available with built-in battery chargers.

Cloth garment bags. Cloth bags, preferred over plastic bags, allow clothes to breathe while still protecting them from insects.

Garment racks. Some racks are free-standing and mounted on wheels; others can be mounted on the wall or hung from the ceiling. Use them to hang clothes in your laundry area or to store off-season clothes.

Pegboard. Made from pressed cardboard, sheets of pegboard have holes that can be fitted with hooks, small shelves, and other hardware for holding tools of all kinds. Pegboard can be screwed or nailed onto drywall or over studs on an unfinished wall, and it can be painted.

Racks, brackets, hangers, and hooks. Versatile and indispensable, these accessories for mounting on walls or ceilings are designed to accommodate an infinite array of items: bicycles, lawn mowers, ladders, garden hose, work clothes, lumber, shop tools, extension cords, ironing board, and iron. Some storage systems, like those for sports equipment, combine baskets, racks, and hooks in a single unit.

Recycling bins and racks. Although many municipalities supply recycling bins, you may want to organize your bottles, plastics, and newspapers in bins or racks kept in your garage or basement before setting materials out for pickup.

Sheds. Ready-made sheds, available in many sizes, shapes, and styles, can be placed in your yard and used for tools if you are short of storage space in your basement or garage. The shed can be outfitted with many of the accessories on this list.

Shelving. Aesthetics need not determine which storage furniture you use, but sturdiness is key. Whether you make or purchase wood shelving or buy metal shelving, set it on the floor or mount it on the wall, be sure it is strong and stable enough to support what you will be storing.

Small-parts organizers. These units, made in various sizes, have banks of small drawers for hardware. You may also find them useful for holding craft supplies.

Storage containers. Choose the kind you need based on the items you're storing—airtight, waterproof containers for important papers, transparent containers for belongings you want to see readily, open bins for sports equipment, cedar-lined trunks for clothing and bedding.

Tool carts, boxes, organizers, and caddies. Some containers are made for specific tools, such as gardening tools, though you can use them for any purpose. Carts, because they are portable, are ideal for tools that you need in the garden or in your driveway to work on your car but also must keep organized in a garage or basement. Some boxes and organizers have small compartments for hardware.

Workbenches. You can build or buy pre-assembled workbenches of all sizes and descriptions. Some come with drawers and/or bottom cabinets for storing tools, hardware, and other supplies.

RESOURCES

RESOURCES

RESOURCES

Looking for a CD storage solution? A new nightstand? Some stacking boxes? The resources in this section will get you started.

Alstergren & Lansell Pty Ltd
Australia
03 9510 6985
Diaries/calendars

• • •

At a Glance
888 302 4155
www.ataglance.com
Calendars/planning products

• • •

Austral Self Storage
Australia
02 9387 5522
www.australselfstorage.com.au
Self-storage

• • •

Bamix
Australia
02 9369 5485
Kitchenware

• • •

Basic Essentials
Australia
02 9328 1227
Kitchenware

• • •

Bed Bath & Beyond
800 462 3966
www.bedbathandbeyond.com
Home/storage organization

• • •

Bed Bath 'n' Table
Australia
03 9387 3322
Home/storage organization

• • •

Binz-The Container Store
416 690 4611
Canada
Home/storage organization

• • •

Bodum
800 232 6386
www.bodum.com
Kitchen storage products

• • •

Broadway Panhandler
212 966 3434
www.broadwaypanhandler.com
Specialty cookware/knife storage

• • •

California Closets
800 274 6754
www.calclosets.com
Closet organization/design

• • •

Casabella
800 841 4140
www.casabella.com
Home/storage organization

• • •

CD Storehouse
800 829 4203
CD storage solutions

• • •

Collins Debden Pty Ltd
Australia
03 9419 6661
Diaries/calendars

• • •

The Container Store
800 786 7315
www.containerstore.com
Home/storage organization

• • •

Crate & Barrel
800 572 5750
www.crateandbarrel.com
Home/storage organization

• • •

Exposures
800 222 4947
www.exposuresonline.com
Photo storage

• • •

Filofax
www.filofax.com
Calendars/daily planners

• • •

Freedom Bag
877 573 3366
www.freedombag.com
Makeup/jewelry organization

• • •

Frontgate
800 626 6488
www.frontgate.com
Home/storage organization

• • •

Gempler's
800 382 8473
www.gemplers.com
Tool storage

• • •

Gracious Home
800 338 7809
www.gracioushome.com
Home/storage organization

• • •

Hammacher Schlemmer
800 321 1484
www.hammacher.com
Home organization

• • •

Hold Everything
800 421 2264
www.holdeverything.com
Closet storage products

• • •

Holy Sheet Fitzroy
Australia
03 9417 0288
www.holysheet.com.au
Home organization

• • •

Home Depot
800 430 3376
www.homedepot.com
Home-improvement products

• • •

Ikea
www.ikea.com
Home organization

• • •

The Ink Pad
212 463 9876
www.theinkpadnyc.com
Personalized ink stamps

• • •

Itoya of America
800 628 4811
www.itoya.com
Home-office organization

• • •

Levenger
800 544 0880
www.levenger.com
Home-office organization

• • •

Light Impressions
800 828 6216
www.lightimpressions.com
Archival storage products

• • •

MacPhee's Wine Cellarage
Australia
03 9696 5200
www.macphees.com
Wine storage

• • •

MINIMAX
Australia
800 260 022
www.minimax.com.au
Kitchen/housewares

• • •

Museum of Useful Things
www.themut.com
Home organization

• • •

OfficeMax
800 788 8080
www.officemax.com
Home-office storage/organization

• • •

Officeworks
Australia
03 9236 1900
www.officeworks.com.au
Home-office organization

• • •

The Organiser Shop
Australia
03 9639 3633
Diaries

• • •

Penhalluriack's Building & Garden Supplies
Australia
03 9523 6000
Garage organization

• • •

Poliform
888 765 4367
www.poliformusa.com
Closet design

• • •

Polestar Calendars
Canada
www.polestar-calendars.com
Family and business calendars

• • •

Pomegranate
800 227 1428
www.pomegranate.com
Calendars

• • •

Pottery Barn
888 779 5176
www.potterybarn.com
Home/storage organization

• • •

Racor
800 783 7725
www.racorinc.com
Garage organization

• • •

Restoration Hardware
800 762 1005
www.restorationhardware.com
Home organization

• • •

Rubbermaid
888 895 2110
www.rubbermaid.com
Home/storage organization

• • •

SecurAway
Australia
03 9681 9991
www.securaway.com.au
Self-storage

• • •

Stacks and Stacks
800 761 5222
www.stacksandstacks.com
Home/storage organization

• • •

Staples
800 333 3330
www.staples.com
Home-office organization

• • •

Storage King
Australia
03 9427 1444
www.storageking.com.au
Home storage

Surry Office National
Australia
02 9211 3399
www.officenational.com.au
Office supplies

Talas
212 219 0770
www.talasonline.com
Archival storage products

Techline
800 697 7573
www.techlineStudio.com
Home/office design

Transtherm Australia Pty Ltd
Australia
02 8399 3500
www.transtherm.com
Wine organization/storage

Tupperware
800 366 3800
www.tupperware.com
Kitchen storage

The Wine Enthusiast
Australia
800 356 8466
www.wineenthusiast.com
Wine organization/storage

Ultimate Home Storage
800 397 7566
www.ultimatechristmas.com
Holiday ornament storage

Umbra
800 327 5122
www.umbra.com
Home/storage organization

Williams-Sonoma
877 812 6235
www.williamssonoma.com
Home/storage organization

Z Gallerie
800 358 8288
www.Zgallerie.com
Home/storage organization

INDEX

Remotes, 76

Rolodex files, 107

Dedication

With much love to my husband, Sam, and my children, Alyson and Andrew. Xoxo

— Meryl Starr

Acknowledgments

I am forever grateful to all those that have guided and supported me.

To Mikyla Bruder for helping me make a dream become a reality, for believing in me, having foresight, great vision, patience, creativity, for being a fabulous editor and a wonderful person to work with.

To Noah Lukeman, my agent, for reading my proposal and believing it could and would turn into something great—I appreciate all your great efforts.

To all my clients past and present for inviting me into your homes, for trusting me, for sharing your personal space and the most intimate areas of your lives, thanks for letting me do what I truly love.

To my dear friend Elyse—I thank you a gazillion times for your constant support, love, friendship, and for being the kind of friend everyone should be lucky enough to have.

To Randi—I am so glad we organized your kitchen on that snowy day back in March of '93, and thanks to you Steven for giving me the idea and encouragement to start my own organizing company.

Alyson and Andrew—thank you for being the best children a mother could ever ask for. I am so lucky.

Sam—thank you for your incredible love and support throughout this entire project, I certainly could not have done it without you.

To all of you that will read this book, it is my hope that it will guide and inspire you to create a home in which you will flourish, improve the quality of your life, and be very happy.

— Meryl Starr

This project would not have been possible without the generosity, support, and hard work of the people who contributed to this book. I would like to express my heartfelt gratitude to the following:

Anthony Albertus, for his keen sense of style and positive outlook; Deborah Sherman, photo assistant extraordinaire; Ben Shaykin at Chronicle Books for the opportunity to work on this project; Keith Sheets for his endless patience and support. Extra thanks to the following people for welcoming us into their homes with such kindness and hospitality: Jules Campfield, Elizabeth Canady, Deborah Bowman, and Carol Knorp.

— Wendi Nordeck

BIOS

Meryl Starr is the owner of Let's Get Organized, a New York–based company that specializes in personal organizing. Her tips and ideas for home organizing have appeared in numerous magazines, including *Woman's Day, Seventeen,* and *In Style.*

Wendi Nordeck is a San Francisco–based commercial photographer specializing in still life, editorial, and advertising. Her work has appeared in numerous publications, including *Bon Appétit; Health; O, The Oprah Magazine; Sunset;* and *Victoria.*